Half Remembered

POETRY
by Peter Davison

The Breaking of the Day (1964)
The City and the Island (1966)
Pretending to Be Asleep (1970)
Dark Houses (1971)

Edward and Natalie Davison at the time
of their marriage, April, 1926.

Half
Remembered

A PERSONAL HISTORY

Peter Davison

HEINEMANN: LONDON

William Heinemann Ltd.

15 Queen Street, Mayfair, London WIX 8BE
LONDON   MELBOURNE   TORONTO
JOHANNESBURG   AUCKLAND

First published by Harper & Row, 1973
First published in Great Britain, 1973
Copyright © by Peter Davison 1973

SBN 434 17920 5

Printed in the United States of America

For Lesley who helped live it
and Jane who helped make it

Contents

"It is the acceptance of . . . one's one and only life cycle as something that had to be and that, by necessity, permitted of no substitutions: it thus means a new, a different love of one's parents. . . . For he knows that an individual life is the accidental coincidence of but one life cycle with but one segment of history; and that for him all human integrity stands or falls with the one style of integrity of which he partakes."

Erik H. Erikson, Childhood and Society

That I should live like one teased by a song,
Some tune half-lost that haunts him all night long;
And O how irrecoverably sweet
Were the forgotten words that went with it.

Edward Davison, "Something Forgotten"

"Everyone is partly their ancestors; just as
everyone is partly man and partly woman."

Virginia Woolf, in a letter to an
unidentified correspondent

PROLOGUE

The Losing Struggle

Here by the sea I cannot see as far as the mountains,
Nor do they loom over my shoulder as they once did.

P. D., "The Losing Struggle"

1.

Home was the compartment of music and of discord, the
vessel of my mother's influence, the rostrum for my father's
voice. Home lay at the instep of the Rocky Mountains, secure
with pinnacles at its back and the Colorado prairies out front.
Before the age of seven, my childhood had been that of the
literary/academic itinerant: two years in Brooklyn Heights;
fifteen months in London, Vienna, and Alassio; two years in
Peekskill and a year in Ossining, New York; six months in
Miami; and, beginning when I was seven, a succession of
rented houses in Boulder, Colorado.

Even after my parents found a home they took frequent
expeditions by car. We drove from Florida to Colorado
through the Dust Bowl in the spring of 1935, and to Utah
and back that same summer. Most Christmases we traveled
away from Boulder and back by car: to Arizona in 1935 and
1937; to Louisiana and Mississippi in 1936; to California in
1939; and, by train, at Easter, to New York in 1938 and 1939.
In the summers we drove to Wyoming or New Mexico or the
western slope of the Rocky Mountains. My mother and my
sister and I were vacationing in a tourist cabin by the river at
Glenwood Springs, Colorado, when war broke out on September 1, 1939. My father had stayed home to complete the

collation of his *Collected Poems.* But in 1937, when I was nine, we settled, seemingly for all time, in our own granite house on a broad street in Boulder. The house is no longer standing, and only two of the family who lived there are still alive.

In Colorado water was the most precious commodity. Snow clung to the mountaintops almost all the year, but on the plains to the east, the air was so dry and the light so sharp that the drifts of a blizzard could melt away in a matter of hours. Summer afternoons sometimes moistened the air with brief thundershowers, but the soil looked baked out an hour later. My childhood was one long quest for water. In the dawn hours of July Wednesdays I rose to patrol the streets where I delivered copies of *Collier's* magazine. On other mornings I roamed across the grassy campus of the University of Colorado, where my father taught English literature. Before the sun struck it, the asphalt of University Avenue gleamed with dew. My bicycle tires hissed through the film of moisture as gently as a garter snake. The trees and flowers shivered as the dawn touched them and they gave up their thin moisture to the sun.

Boulder stands at the edge of the Great Plains, where a thousand miles of prairie abruptly cants upward into the foothills of the Rocky Mountains. The town faces east along the fortieth parallel of north latitude. Mountains—a high screen of pink granite cliffs and crumbling ochre sandstone swathed in dark evergreens—shelter its back from the incessant westerly winds. The melt from a glacier twenty miles away drained down into our reservoir. Lawns and flowers had to be watered almost daily. When I returned from my early morning rambles on Tuesdays, Thursdays, and Saturdays (the days when our side of the street was allowed to water its gardens) , it was my chore to turn on the hoses and shift the sprinklers from place to place.

After this, at eight o'clock, I joined a garble of little boys at the university's indoor swimming pool—its "Natatorium." Every morning we were allotted an hour to teach ourselves to swim. We hurled ourselves naked and dripping from the diving board or thrashed up and down the length of the chlorinated tank. In the afternoons, the same boys, carrying bathing suits, would meet at the Hygienic Swimming Pool, a larger, plainer public place under a wooden roof downtown, operated as an adjunct of the Hygienic Ice Company. Here girls swam too. Beneath the vast shed of the roof the water gave off lulling green refractions of sensuality. The girls' dressing room had holes gouged in its wooden partitions. When we could, we peeped at the girls undressing and breathed harder in the chlorinated air. When we came out, our eyes turned first to the ten-meter diving board at the deep end. Bold or exhibitionistic boys might fling themselves from this enormous height, a free hand waving high while the other held the nose. They squeezed their eyes shut as they cannoned into the water. The girls pretended not to notice who jumped, but they certainly singled out those who didn't. I was one of the few who, having dared to climb the endless ladder and stare appalled at the unthinkable water below, had the cowardice to slink back down again. Rankling with self-disgust at my failure of nerve, I decided on an even sterner test—to execute a perfectly flat racing dive in two feet of water. I broke my nose on the bottom. The pugilist's knob that resulted was a permanent object of pride.

Its campus was so big that the university had to arrange for its own irrigation supply, which it tapped by a series of canals and ditches from the clouded upstream waters of Boulder Creek. (Glacier water, crystal and potable, was too good for large-scale irrigation.) By the side of every slate-paved path on the university grounds ran two small irrigation ditches a foot deep. Student athletes on "scholarship" tended the ditches during the summers, keeping them clear of weeds, sliding boards into concrete slots to block their flow and sluice their water to the lawns. After the morning hour at the Natatorium I would stand by to assist Packy, a bronzed, slope-shouldered second baseman. He stood leaning on his shovel in gum boots and a pith helmet, watching the water slide in chuckling sheets over the parched grass. He always smiled at me with brilliant Italian teeth when I arrived.

Across the street from my house lay the stagnant university pond. Pleasantly landscaped with willow, reeds, evergreens, and rhododendrons, it was arched over by a bridge of pink sandstone, the local building material that lent the entire university a mock-Tuscan style. Here I discovered the under-water world, angling with bits of rotting bacon as I lay on a wet belly to lower the bait slowly closer to inching crayfish. Once the prey sank a claw into the bacon and began to gnaw, I held my breath, counted to three, and yanked string, bait, and perhaps crayfish in an arc out onto the muddy bank. There the creature flipped and scuttled until made captive in a pail, where he would eventually die.

Boulder Creek tumbled out of the mountains and arrived near our house bled of its strength, stained with mine tailings and corrupted by minor industrial offal. In the winter its water was diverted to flood four tennis courts for a skating rink. It gathered driftwood along its banks after the spring freshets. Then we fashioned rafts and launched Tom Sawyer voyages of piracy and adventure, though even in spate the creek (pronounced *crick*) seldom had enough depth to float us more than a hundred yards on the waterlogged limbs we huddled together with string and rusty nails. We lurked

along its banks in the thickets of willow and dwarf cotton-
wood, where with homemade bows and arrows we aspired to
kill game. In the underbrush we could track the spoor of
college love affairs. We also tried to fish for trout with
bamboo poles. Later we acquired professional fly rods with
catgut leaders, boughten Royal Coachmen, and eventually
home-tied dry flies. By the side of the creek lived a red-
headed boy my age, unruly and rumored to be "adopted,"
who instructed me, with diminishing degrees of success, in
the mysteries of the Oz books, root beer making, fly tying,
buggery, and tattooing. I was as frightened of him as a
chicken of a snake.

The most forbidding of the flatland waters was Baseline
Lake, which by its very vastness fell in a category beyond the
others. It lay out on the prairie three miles east of town
along a ribbon of corrugated dirt road with red-winged
blackbirds or meadowlarks singing from every fencepost.
This road ran straight along the fortieth parallel until it
encountered the bank of an artificial lake, a mile across. Baseline Lake was tinted yellow with silt. It had muddy beachlike
banks. On summer afternoons we went there for family
swimming expeditions or picnics. It was big enough for
boats, wide enough to be a challenge to cross.

One day my parents' friend Robert Penn Warren tucked
his red hair into a slippery black bathing cap, plugged his
ears and nose, lowered his lean barrel-chested swimmer's
body into the water, and set out swimming across the yellow
lake in a churning slow crawl which never relented. He
gradually receded from sight, and I could hardly see his head
any longer when he suddenly rose out of the water at the far
bank, a mile away. He lifted his hands to adjust his bathing
cap or his nose plug, and then, without pausing longer than
half a minute, lowered himself back into the water and began

his steady trudgen back. When he emerged at our shore a while later, he pulled off his bathing cap to reveal again the familiar hawklike head of our young friend, breathing easy. I had known that he was a nice man, but not that he could do *that*. I was amazed. No one, not Packy, not Wilfred, the hired man who had let me ride a plowhorse when I was four and taught me to sing "I Ain't Got No Use for the Women," had ever inflamed such admiration in me as this prodigious swimmer. I practiced for two years afterwards till I could swim across the lake myself, shifting every hundred strokes from crawl to back to side to breast, aided by the presence of an accompanying boat. When I finally achieved the crossing and the return, a dream of my earlier childhood came true, a dream in which I crossed the water and reached my mother on the other side.

2.

The flatland waters were as nothing to those of their country of origin, the living rocks and snows of the mountains. In my eighth summer my family went to Utah, where my father was to teach at the summer school of Brigham Young University. The town of Provo turned out to be riddled with scarlet fever and measles, so my mother took my sister Lesley and me to a log cabin high in the mountains, where my father could come at night and weekends. The rough shack lay on the side of a valley looking across to Mount Timpanogos. For some weeks we lived there in the woods under the green mass of the mountain. Every pail of water for drinking or cooking had to be carried by hand or hauled on an arrangement of pulleys from a rocky spring a hundred feet down the slope. The water boiled at less than two hundred degrees because of the altitude, and everything took longer to cook than usual.

After this I began to be drawn by the mountains, the westward magnetism of the high places, the pull of the peaks and plateaus lying above the plains, the streams full of jeweled trout, the cabins and mine shafts and crumbling relics of the 1859 Colorado gold fever, and finally the upper reaches beyond timberline where there was nothing but rock, snow, and sky. Far above the plains lay other lakes of emerald or jade nestled in the groin of a mountainside, lakes of sapphire and turquoise gathered at the toe of a glacier or palisaded by evergreens.

At twelve, a friend and I constructed a hut of saplings and thatched it with matted pine needles. It lay in a hollow behind one of the Flatirons, just off the main trail a mile or so above Boulder, but so camouflaged that no passer-by could have spotted it. We took pride in its four tiny "rooms," in which we would peck and poke and crouch as though they were nests.

My Cub Scout pack took a hike to the head of the Arapaho glacier itself, the source of all Boulder's water. The trail wound up through forests of Douglas fir, blue spruce, and the perfumes of conifers. The path echoed to our feet as we ascended among the tall trees. Rooted far down the slope, they caught the dazzling alpine sunlight in their top branches, at the level of our eyes. As we climbed, the trees shrank, and eventually scrub juniper replaced them altogether. Then timber line, a rubble of rock, patches of snow. Our voices dried and hoarsened from breathing the sparse air. Over the last ridge, at eleven thousand feet, we crossed a rounded crest.

The glacier dangled below us like an unbleached bib, embraced by mountains. It was not a new glacier. The mountains were winning; it was melting faster than it moved. Its lower lip grazed forward over its own moraine in the cold months and retreated back again when the summer came to warm it. Shadows lay across the surface like furrows on an old man's face—crevasses, some visible, some concealed and treacherous. Where snow had melted from the surface, rocks and the stains of gravel cropped out. Here and there pink streaks, "watermelon snow," were discolored by red algae which grew under the surface. The pink snow was said to make you sick if you ate it.

As we stared down the length of the vast apron we ate our sandwiches and wondered how the watermelon snow could make us sick. Then, under our scout leader's nervous eye, we went running and sliding down the upper slopes of the glacier. We were powerfully drawn by its mighty downward weight. Could we ride it downhill? Could we have urged the great cold creature to shoulder the mountains aside like clouds and burst through the foothills with water for the brown plains below? Something restrained us, our secret suspicions that this great smutted elephant of ice was not to be believed after all, that it might only be a sullied leftover of last winter's storms rather than the frozen reservoir we had imagined. Surely nothing so unremarkable as this monstrous thing could really be the source of life, the source of water?

3.

At sixteen, I penetrated as far into the West as I had the strength for. After five years of practice in mountain climbing and a record of ascending a dozen peaks over thirteen thousand feet, I set out with a master from my boarding school in charge of me and two other students to climb the highest peak in the Crestone group in southern Colorado. The northern face had, we believed, not often been climbed before. We camped for the night by the side of a lake at ten thousand feet. After a breakfast of porridge, bacon, and cocoa, we set out to climb four thousand feet to the summit of the Crestone Needle, up the side of the cirque that a vanished glacier had scoured out long ago. By midmorning we four had reached the high-ice mark of the glacier and begun to grapple with the naked conglomerate outcroppings of granite and quartz that made up the body of the mountain.

The ledges were far apart. Our pace slowed as we found breath hard to catch and as the climb took us in the thighs and arms. Our bare fingers scraped against the stone for handholds. At the steepest of the ledges we were brought to a halt before a crack where two rock shields met edge to edge, tilted almost vertical, leaving only the barest of angles between their surfaces. In this situation there was only room for three to climb. The others worked above me, maneuvering for an hour or more on the rope to inch back and forth with their chests close to the rock. As the weakest climber I was left to sit below. There was nothing for me to do but glance up at the nerve-wracking struggle above me, or else to let my view fall through half a mile of space to the azure water of the tiny lake where we had camped. I stared down, pretending not to hear the scrape and gasping of the climbers working above. As time passed I began to shiver. I was reminded of the diving platform at the Hygienic Pool, but now there was no way for me to climb down, no way for me to go higher without the help of the others.

The noises of the climbers' boot soles scrabbling against the rock, the pauses to retie the rope, the murmurs of instruction and response, grew gradually louder and began to ring in my ears. I found I was sitting at the edge of the cliff as casually as in a chair with my legs dangling over. What was I thinking of? I shrank away from the abyss, shivering harder. I crouched as close as I could to the rock face. I nuzzled into the shoulder of the mountain. Time slowed and slowed. The noises above receded. How soon would the bodies of the other climbers begin to float past, one by one, like balloons?

After an immeasurable length of time the impasse above me was overcome, but by then I was all but paralyzed. The other climbers had to haul me up the first rock face like a sack of grain. After a time I made my arms and legs work again, and they negotiated overhangs, ascents with piton and pulley, tall rock chimneys which required bracing feet against one side, back against the other, and shimmying up. I gradually recovered control, inching along between the other climbers. We reached the sloping scree of the summit and found under a cairn in a steel cylinder the paper where previous climbers had recorded their routes and the dates. We set ourselves down as the third party ever to have climbed the north route.

Then we staggered down the mountain the easy round-about way, ninety minutes to camp after six or seven hours ascending. I needed no help now, in fact I ran ahead of the others. We quickly struck camp and walked out past the lake through the woods several miles to where the car would meet us at dusk. The shade of the firs, the metallic gurgle of the brook beside the path, the thickening darkness, hid the pallor of my face, my shaking knees, my trembling voice.

The Continental Divide is an imaginary line that runs down the backbone of the Rocky Mountains, separating the watersheds of east-running streams from those that run off to the west. I had been turned back from it, had turned away from the presumed quest for purity and solitude. "Something we were withholding made us weak," as Frost puts it, "Until we found out that it was ourselves/ We were withholding. . . ." I took the searing terror of that climb as a sort of signal that my destiny lay behind me in the East. I did not know then how many American Westerners had turned back toward the sea to put their origins to use in Boston, New York, New Hampshire, London, Rye, Paris, Rapallo, Rome. The great photographs of the early frontier are preserved in Eastern museums and libraries. Westerners who arrive in the East must contend with the sea, "Mighty Manhattan, with spires, and the sparkling and hurrying tides," the Quaker graveyard at Nantucket, the yawning and imperious depths of the past.

The creature who had been defeated by the mountains was the child in myself, who knew fear and could not help shrinking from it, a manikin who would walk always beside my adult self, who might never be outgrown, and who had existed long before I crawled up the heights of the Crestones. This child had learned about fear and pain where everyone learns about such things, from his parents. Santayana calls parents the child's natural enemies: "They *are* his natural enemies, just as the winds and the sea and wild animals are. They are necessary and useful to him in the same sense. But they are not his friends. They do not will anything as he wills it."

Part One

Part One

I

Natural Enemies

Returning now, I walk through open reaches
Naked to all, where I must once have lain
As warm as a rabbit's beating heart
In a thicket sprinkled with morning, where each leaf
Burned green, hot as a newly-minted coin.

> P. D., "True Feeling Leaves No Memory"

He asks
me how I came to this place and
this work, and I tell him how
I began with animals, and
he tells me how
he began with animals.   We
talk about growing up and losing
the strange things we never
understood and settling.

> Philip Levine, "Angel Butcher"

1.

When I was three, in 1931, my family lived near Peekskill, New York. My father, who earned his living as a lecturer, was often away from home. My mother, my baby sister, and I lived with our Viennese nurse in a rented house with a few acres of hilly hayfields, an orchard, a vegetable garden, a pond, and the ruins of a gristmill. The pond was not far from the house. One passed the low-lying timbers of the rotting mill, turned to the right behind them to cross a millstream on stepping stones, and followed a path up the opposite bank past the milldam to a tiny boathouse and a small dock where a canoe and a tub of a rowboat were moored. Across the pond loomed islands and other less comprehensible bits of geography which my father labeled *peninsula, promontory, isthmus, strait.* In the winter, when we could slide or skate across the ice, the pond seemed smaller, but in summertime, when I was immersed low in the cool dark water, with frogs croaking around its edge, the other side seemed as far away as England. In my fourth summer I somehow managed to set out alone in the rowboat bound for the magnet of the island opposite. It could not have been much of a distance, but it was too far for me. I struggled for what seemed hours, paddling mostly in circles, and though I came close enough to recognize the trees and rocks that I might touch and walk on, I simply could not make the boat reach land. Bobbing and thrusting in the boat while water sloshed over its leaky flat bottom, I was rescued by my mother in the canoe and scolded—whether for attempting to reach the other side or for not succeeding, I could not be sure.

There were long summer afternoons when friends or family, my New York grandparents, my aunt and young cousins from Scarsdale, my parents' friends in black jersey bathing suits, swam and lolled on the dock. My mother, a strong swimmer with a good scissors kick and a pretty overarm motion, filled me with longing and envy when she swam away from the dock across the pond, emerged on the faraway rocks, and waved from the other side. My feeling of helplessness at being stranded on the near shore was sharpened by my fear that some monster, perhaps even so kindly a beast as Small Porgies in the *Just-So Stories*, might engorge her from the depths, and I would be left alone by the waterside with Schwester our nurse and Lesley my sister, with no one to guide me surely past the dangers that lurked along the path home. Danger in this sense was manmade: the leaky boats, the rusty nails in the boathouse that with a scratch could poison my blood, the rich brown decaying boards of the gristmill that might give way and plunge me into some fetid cellar, the barbed wire on a fence, a treacherous stepping stone. My mother tried to teach me to swim, holding me in her arms to make me kick and splash the water with my hands, my eyes squeezed shut against the wet; or drying me firmly with a sun-warmed towel. The feel of her hands and the towel scrubbing my back and shoulders is still with me, from the pondside dock or after my bath.

I was a frail child. How could anyone expect me to learn to swim? I *felt* frail. My mind raced inside my body, but my body was unable to keep up. I had in fact often been ill—at two years with an infantile dietary deficiency diagnosed as celiac disease, then with a spot of tuberculosis, and later, in the Peekskill winters, with pneumonia and otitis. My mother, heeding my ears more than my fears, didn't press me to learn to swim. I learned early that illness could serve me in many ways. Not only could it shield me when I felt afraid, but it was the surest way of attracting my mother's attention. She had a high Jewish regard for doctors, like her mother before her, and I was carried off to the examining table at the scratch of a throat or the twitch of an eye. My diet, in the fashion of the day, was doled out at implacable intervals, and as I grew older I found that, though I was praised for emptying my plate, I got more notice by toying with a full one. At the suspicion of poor appetite I was swathed and swaddled, embrocated and spoon fed. Help was never far away. Even at night if I uttered a faint cry, my mother came to me—more quickly when my father was not at home.

Ingratiating myself with my father was a different problem, one that called for achievement. A new scrawl, a nursery rhyme learned for recitation, recognition of the letters of the alphabet—these were what was wanted. To please my father I must act more an adult than I felt; to tug at my mother I must act more the child. I called my mother Mummy till the end of her life, but I soon began calling my father by his nickname, Teddie, as though he were an equal, or a rival. One day when I was four he ceased to be Daddy and took on his new name. He had been traveling and returned during the night. My sister and I ran into our parents' bedroom to greet him as soon as we were awake. They lay side by side in their beds. I instantly realized that I did not want this man for a "Daddy," and announced that Lesley and I would henceforward call him by my mother's name for him. I expected this declaration to come as a shock, but to my surprise both parents seemed pleased. I was amazed that they did not suspect my motives.

Lesley was two years younger than I, and healthy as a puppy. It was therefore easy for me to outdo her both in frailty and in precocity. I could use either weapon, or, when absolutely necessary, both, and I developed ingenious combinations, like asking, when ill, to have difficult books read aloud to me. My first successful trial of skill and cunning was the besting of our Austrian nurse, "Schwester" Benedikt, though I cannot recall now precisely how the thing was done. Schwester was a Viennese, of early middle age. My parents had hired her when we lived, briefly, abroad, and she had gladly accepted the chance to come to America and leave behind the blind alleys of depression Vienna. She took a European line toward child rearing and secretly, sometimes even openly, disapproved of my mother's progressive ways with her children. Though my mother played with us, it was usually Schwester who dressed us in the mornings, roughly tugging on my *lederhosen* or my striped jersey long-sleeved shirts, punishing my lapses into daytime incontinence or nighttime bed-wetting, spanking my *bupsch* when no one, except Lesley, was looking. I gradually developed a detestation of the woman. My advantage over her was my knowledge of English, as hers over me was brute force. I realized that if I were to lie to my mother and exaggerate the extent of Schwester's misdeeds, I would be perfectly safe from discovery. Lesley, only two, knew more German than she did English and was an uncertain witness.

Even so, Schwester was no pushover. My little show-off achievements with language, like the proper pronunciation of *isthmus,* cut no ice with her; and she viewed my illnesses with dark skepticism, to be treated if possible with cold baths, fresh air, and a brisk walk with the Scottish terrier, MacDuff. But her cunning was no match for mine, and I doubt if she ever knew what hit her. One day we were told that she was going to New York, to take up another position tending babies. Even if it had not been my tactics that finished off my first adversary, yet I had been in at the kill.

Now I could sit happily alone with my mother on the porch or on the dock in the sun. She often wore a sort of Barbary costume, slightly piratical in aspect—floppy terra-cotta slacks, frilly white blouse with blue embroidery on the full breast, and a bandanna binding her crisp reddish hair. On winter afternoons, when my father was away and I was very likely to have an earache, I could rally my mother by my attainments as well as my frailties, making her read to me for hours out of fairy tales, or a children's version of the *Odyssey*, on the cover of which Athene looked very much like my mother herself. The powerful bond between us was not yet effectively disputed by my sister, who was too young to tolerate much reading, and whose healthy infant needs were rudimentary by comparison with my own feverish cravings. When Lesley and I were left alone together, we fought; and my explanations, when my mother found her hurt and crying, were paradigms of self-justification.

We often drove into New York in a black De Soto with red-wire-spoked spare wheels carried on the sides behind the front mudguards, to visit my grandparents, or to Scarsdale, where my mother's sister and her husband lived, or to nearby Croton-on-Hudson to visit my parents' dear friends Stanley and Edith Isaacs. We had been shopping, one cold February day after an ice storm, and were driving home from Peekskill. I sat next to my mother. My sister was in the back seat next to a hundred-pound sack of potatoes. It was growing dark. We were descending a steepish slope, and a truck was spinning its wheels up the hill on the opposite side. Our turn off the highway was to the left, and my mother, with snow pelting the windshield and only a hand-operated wiper to deter it, unwisely applied her brakes to slow for the turn. The De Soto began to skid. It sailed slowly towards the roadside edge on the right, and its back wheels broached out into the middle of the road. We slid towards the post-and-cable guard-rails. We struck, caught, and halted. I flew forward and my head, as lightly as buckshot, struck the windshield, which fell apart and released a cold wet wind over my face and neck. I heard the potatoes slide and thud against the back of the seat.

Everything was silent suddenly, but in the gathering darkness I could no longer see. My mother began crying and gulping in the seat on my left, and my sister gurgled, apparently unhurt, in the back. My face was wet. The air was cold. I heard the left-hand door being yanked open, and a scurry of conversation came through. The truck driver had stopped, and his deep voice tried to calm my mother's sobbing. Still blinded, I was lifted from my seat and carried into the leather-and-grease smell of the truck. Lesley, whimpering at the sight of blood, was put on the seat at my side. I heard my mother and the driver grunting with the effort of pushing the crippled De Soto out of the way of traffic. Then the truck started up and moved off, the window open and the cold wind blowing, along the fork towards our house. We left Lesley at home with someone and sped off in the truck to the doctor's, where stitches were taken. I was not badly hurt, only cut on the eyelid and at the corner of the mouth, but I was covered with blood.

It took me a week or two to recover from the indignity of the accident. As my mother quavered over me I came to realize that this round of invalidism could not be laid at *my* door. It had not been my own weakness or valetudinarianism that had brought me low, but my mother's negligence, her bad driving. Despite her breathless endearments I bore cuts on my face, cuts that would heal into scars which, however tiny, I would carry for the rest of my life. How I prized this evidence that I was not to blame. Clearly those one loved could be held responsible for pain, especially women, in this case the woman one loved more than any other person. This was one of the most convenient—and unluckiest—discoveries of my life.

When my father came home from his lecturing, he made much of the haphazard driving—so he designated it—that had led to the crash, the wounding, the wrecking of the car, the exposure of both his children to a winter storm. He too had learned in his childhood to make a woman the scapegoat for miseries he could not comprehend or prevent, and he now passed along some of those lessons to the pallid and suffering victim, who watched him rant at my mother's betrayal (of what? of me?), as the two of them clucked over me alternately, in guilt or righteousness. Teddie, to my sudden surprise, had become my ally in condemning my mother because she had brought me to grief. How very strange. It had always been *she* who protected me from *him*. There was no way of knowing what had possessed her to encompass the accident, or him to condemn it, but it had opened up for me a new theatre of enterprise. In that manikin part of me that parroted information and could babble the language of my elders, I became aware that I held an ace in the game, even though I might never actually have to play it. I had uncovered the sensitive zone of their relationship. To my earlier powers this was a welcome addition of knowledge. I could play, or threaten to play, my new card with equal effect whether embroiled with my father or implicated with my mother. I imagined that sooner or later I could, if I wished, pry them apart, the bad dream of every child.

When my father was at home the weather was usually warm, for the lecturing eased in the summers. Then he wrote in a little cottage above the house in the orchard. In this summer, 1932, I think, he was struggling to write a play that he never finished. And on summer afternoons, beginning about the time I started to call him Teddie, he privileged me to climb the hill through the newly raked hay to knock at his door and be taught to read. This half hour was the great event of each day. I sat by my father's side at his desk, and he tapped out words for me on the typewriter so that I could watch the letters being convened into words which he pronounced for me in his rich English voice. He spoke like no one else I knew, as though he were a priest of the language intoning its rituals, and his recitation endowed the written sentences with solemnity. *Cat, rat, sat, mat; the cat sat on the mat; the cat ran; the cat killed the rat; the cat sat on the mat.* His voice transformed these interesting events into high-pitched drama, reveling in the breadth of the English *a,* while the typewriter assembled the words inch by inch, with a tap for each letter and a gulp for each space. Words and sentences grew before my eyes while they echoed in my ears, and the tension between ear and eye wove the fabric of English. The rhymes acted as mnemonics.

It was an extraordinary method of teaching a child to read, perhaps three decades ahead of its time. Not only did I become adept at an early age, able to read anything that interested me before I ever spent a day in school, but the written word was indissolubly joined to the sound of Teddie's voice. A bond had been sealed between my eye and my ear by his teaching methods, but the training at my father's knee sealed a deeper bond between us that never cracked while we both lived, no matter what other interferences estranged us. He had served as a minister in marrying me to the English language—not the American language, which I had to learn from my mother and elsewhere, but the language of the Tyne, the Cam, and the Thames, of Shakespeare and Blake and Wordsworth, the soft tongue of de la Mare and George Herbert, the rough tongue of Cobbett, the puissant tongue of Dickens, Swift, and Yeats.

My father touched me on the quick of myself, of all my latent capacities as student, learner, editor, or poet. He set a ladder against the wall of language. He showed me not only how to climb it but inculcated the nature of language itself, its capacity for transcending space. He sounded for me the strength of the wood that made up its rungs and the timber of its rails. The uncanny resonances of his voice taught me that the spaces between the rungs and rails were as much part of the ladder as the wood sticks that enclosed them. It was a gift. Ladders can be carried anywhere and climbed wherever there is a surface to stand on and a height to ascend for the building of a wall, the picking of apples, the repair of a temple, for putting out a fire, or fortifying a cave. But language can be used for less worthy purposes than these.

2.

Music, not language, first drew my parents together. They met at a party in London in December 1924, and he walked her home. On their way through the streets, he sang to her. It was his way of impressing new girls and had often been successful before. She no doubt surprised him by joining in his singing. She had already claimed his attention with her auburn hair and her energy, her full body and eager eyes, her readiness to laugh. I imagine he was in love with her before the evening was over, for he was the more susceptible of the two. When she returned to New York, Teddie wrote her almost every day until he sailed for America to claim her in the summer of 1925.

They were the sort of people who sing when they are happy. Though neither had professional training, both had been raised to make music. My father had sung anthems and oratorios as an English boy soprano in South Shields, Newcastle-on-Tyne, and even as far away as Durham. After he left school in his teens he helped manage a music hall, where he learned dozens of Edwardian popular songs as well as the Handel-dominated church music and the favorite operatic airs of the time. My mother, brought up in New York, studied the piano like all good Jewish girls. By the time she went to Barnard College in 1919 she owned and could play a large library of Liszt and Schumann and Beethoven, Debussy and Satie. At intervals in her later life she took up the study of the piano again, once squeaking into a master class conducted by Josef and Rosina Lhevinne in Boulder. I can remember sitting at home maddened by my mother's half-speed repetitions of the "Fantaisie-Impromptu" of Chopin.

Like other people of their generation, my parents took more joy in making music than in listening to it, and the music they enjoyed together was in the nineteenth-century Romantic tradition, especially at times when they were happy together. I loved to watch and hear them sing Schubert and Schumann—"Erlkönig" or "Die Krähe," or "Ich grolle nicht"—while my father sang *forte* and my mother strove to keep up with the harder accompaniments. Once they even prepared a public song recital for performance in Denver at the Cactus Club, and for weeks beforehand they rehearsed. The encore was a comic Irish ballad called "The Cork Leg," about a man whose pegleg ran away with him.

Their musicmaking was naturally more acceptable to a child than their noisy and frequent quarreling, but I suspect that the two activities were for them of equal intimacy.

I wanted to copy their musicmaking. I was set to study the piano for a while, and later the clarinet. But I was a lazy practicer and this, combined with poor finger dexterity, kept me from making remarkable strides with either instrument. Still, my first recognizable public triumph was being chosen concertmaster of my junior high school band in a fair contest with Buddy Hanselman, the son of the florist. We each played, behind a screen, a solo part from a band arrangement of one of the "L'Arlésienne" suites of Bizet.

Our fathers teach us what we should become; our mothers teach us what we are. Teddie sang for us, but my mother sang *with* my sister and me. At our tiniest, she dressed us in *lederhosen* and *dirndls*, and she taught us the German tunes she had learned as a child: "Hopp, hopp, hopp, Pferdchen lauf Galopp!"; "Im Wald und auf der Heide, Da such ich meine Freude. Ich bin ein Jägersmann, Ich bin ein Jägersmann"; "Muss i denn, muss i denn, in Städtele hinaus, Städtele hinaus, und du, mein Schatz, bleibt hier?"

Not only the tunes but the language went unshared by my father. His incapacity to pronounce German (to say nothing of American English) was a joke I eagerly came to share with my mother. During Schwester's rule I had used my knowledge of English to betray her, and afterwards, till I forgot the language, it was German I employed to speak to my mother without Teddie's understanding. At ten I was sent to take twice-weekly German lessons with the wife of a professor at the University of Colorado.

Mrs. Kempner was a frail but forceful little lady who was literally redolent of the Old World. Her house was full of German encyclopedias, little volumes of Mörike and Eichendorff, illustrated books of painting and sculpture, and the scent of lavender. She was a woodcarver and gradually walled her rooms with bas-relief oaken panels. She also collected curiously shaped pieces of pitch pine in the mountains and teased them into abstract shapes. With its Oriental rugs and Venetian glass, its paisleyed and cluttered style, its plates of little cakes and carafe of sweet wine, Mrs. Kempner's house was an outpost of *Mitteleuropa*.

After a year or two of grammar and vocabulary, she took to teaching me Heine and Goethe, or, more often, to learning *Lieder*. I sang, and she accompanied me on an old upright piano with brass sconces for candles attached at either side of the music rack. The little old German lady plinked the keys with her blue-veined hands while I aped my father's stance and piped my soprano in emulation of his huge tenor: "Mir graust es, wenn ich sein Antlitz sehe . . ." In May 1940, just as France was falling, we reached our zenith of pretension with Lohengrin's narrative, "In fernem Land, uhn nahbar euren Schritten. . . ." It was unlikely, it was preposterous, yet both of us were in deadly earnest.

Thirty years later, just before she died at a great age, Mrs. Kempner wrote me a long and touching letter about the meaning of those lessons to her. But they had meant no less to me, though my motive was less obvious than either she or I then suspected. I never learned any instrument properly, only singing; and I learned German only to the point of being able to pronounce and possess the words of the songs I might wrest away from my father and sing at my mother's side.

Coming home from school, or from playing "telephone" in Buddy Hanselman's father's greenhouse, or from sliding on the snows of the university campus, I entered my mother's house as a traveler enters an oasis. There is no reproducing the quality of a contented household. It emanates from the furniture and the walls, each rug says all is well. Silence and the murmur of kitchen noises equally express it. The hall of our house was dressed in the very "modern" wallpaper my mother had ordered in New York on an annual trip. By the foot of the stairs stood the mahogany cellaret, holding the liquor supply where it could be got at easily. It also had a built-in humidor for cigars. The books kept on the hall shelves included *Swann's Way, The Tale of Genji, Joseph and His Brothers,* presumably because they were all "foreign" and therefore did not belong among the English literature in my father's large study on the top floor.

The living room was large enough for parties (of which there were many). It had a gold sofa and a gray one, and armchairs, and a Victorian horsehair loveseat backed into the front window. Over the fireplace hung an oil painting by Ernest Fiene, a great bouquet of purple lilacs in a glass vase standing in front of a gray Venus de Milo. Under it, directly on the white plaster wall, Boardman Robinson late one night had crayoned a self-portrait. The shining Steinway dominated the other end of the room like a Grail. I could climb on the piano bench and peek inside at the signatures on the sounding board of visiting musicians who had played on it— Percy Grainger, Harold Bauer, Josef Lhevinne, Rosina Lhevinne, Ernst Bacon, Josef Raieff, and the others who came to give concerts at the university and often stayed in our house.

My father might be sitting in the big maroon-colored corduroy armchair smoking his pipe and nursing a drink, though sometimes he went upstairs to his study and the sound of the typewriter could be heard. Our wire-haired terrier, Scruts, lay under the piano if he was at home, or else kept my sister company in her room, where she wrote articles for her family newspaper, *Davison Doings,* or compiled end-less lists of names.

Beatrice Tafoya, our Mexican maid (the euphemism of the day was "Spanish-American"), was one of thirteen children in a family of sugar beet workers. She lived with us from the time she was seventeen until she married a stockyards worker named Bob Lucero and moved to Denver. She had bad buck teeth, which she hid with her hand when embarrassed, and uncertain eyesight. She became a superb cook and, as the oldest of her immense family, knew all about children. She had her own bedroom and bathroom at the back of the house. In addition to her room and board she earned a better-than-average ten dollars a week cash, which was 15 percent of my father's income before taxes. She cooked, she cleaned, she served at table, she washed the dishes, she dealt with us children, she did everything but the shopping and the laundry, which was washed and ironed on Mondays by Mrs. Clemens in the basement. Beatrice went to visit her family on Sundays and on Thursday afternoons, and they drove her home in their old solid-wheeled Chevrolet with brothers and sisters hanging out of every window. My sister and I adored her. She loved us but aspired to nothing for us, or for herself. The aspirations of the house went on up front, out there in the living room among the pictures and the furniture and the music, where the news of the Spanish Civil War and the speeches of Hitler threatening Czechoslovakia came out of the huge walnut-veneered radio cabinet with its green eye for fine tuning.

When I came home from school, was my mother in the kitchen with Beatrice, or, more likely, talking on the telephone? Or out? It did not matter. Wherever she was, even if she was away East, in New York, this was her house, no one else's, and the presences of the rest of us in it, while necessary to the atmosphere, could never take it from her. Whatever voices we raised in its shelter, whether in song or laughter or quarrel, she was at attention in every framed lithograph and Oriental rug, in the antique cobbler's bench in front of the gray sofa, in the painting of lilacs over the fireplace, in the gauzy white curtains, in the massive many-legged dining room table and its heavy matching sideboards, in the smells of pot roast coming from the kitchen, or in the sight of live lilacs from the dining room window. Years later, after my mother's death, I took my wife to Boulder to visit the house and found that it had just been pulled down. There was no trace of the past in the ruins except, on one chunk of plaster, a scrap of my mother's silver-on-white 1937 wallpaper.

3.

If my parents sang when they were happy, they quarreled when they were not. Loudly, vengefully, often. My mother came from a family in which the women dominated the men in social position and education. The pattern was characteristically American: a young man emigrated from Europe (the Palatinate or Vienna or Austro-Hungary) to avoid conscription or escape the hardships of a large peasant family. He came to New York or Saint Louis in 1848 or 1870 or 1890, got into some sort of commerce through a cousin, and in time set up a business of his own. Then he looked about for a wife and settled on the daughter of some man who, a generation earlier, had done the same thing. The girl would have been trained by an English-speaking mother and would have attended genteel American schools, learning the piano and French in order to wash away the Plattdeutsch or Yiddish her father spoke. Her mother would have guided her education, clothes, and comportment, until the day when her father, still speaking English with a marked accent, would bring home a promising and prosperous young man.

For four or five generations my mother's forebears had followed this cycle. Their names were all German, all the sorts of names given to Jews during the latter Diaspora: Cullmann, Herzog, Weiner, Pappenheimer, Blum. My grandfather Joseph Solomon Weiner came from the small village of Trenčín, in Slovakia, to New York at the age of seventeen, in a steerage berth paid for by his older brothers, who had found a foothold in the cotton goods business. Ten years or so afterwards he had prospered enough to be tempted by the charms of Charlotte Herzog, a young redhead who was visiting relatives in Woodmere, Long Island.

Lottie had been born in Memphis in 1871 and could remember the great yellow fever epidemics, when the plague swept up the Mississippi from New Orleans, and everyone who could afford to, left town till it was past. Her father, Herman Herzog (an evasive if indecisive man noted mainly for his ingenuity in having deserted from both sides during the War Between the States), began in the tobacco business in Memphis but tired of the climate and sold his share of the enterprise to his wife's brothers, the Cullmanns, who ran it thereafter with enormous success from New York.

In Saint Louis, where the family settled, Herman Herzog went into wholesale dry goods. For a while he could not go wrong, but he loathed the trade and suffered unmethodical business practices which brought him acute dyspepsia until the day he died, in his nineties. His indigestion had become intolerable some time before that, so he unloaded the whole-sale store on his only son, Fred Herzog, my grandmother's brother, who hated it as much as his father had. Fred sold out the business in 1919, when he was in his forties, and lived comfortably on the proceeds for the next forty-nine years, marrying several times with indifferent success, traveling a lot for pleasure, and occasionally painting a watercolor. In 1968 he died without issue, and enough of his well-husbanded fortune came to me to enable me to buy an old farmhouse with a piece of land in Gloucester, Massachusetts.

There are no Herzogs in Saint Louis any longer. During my great-grandparents' heyday in the 1890s, they lived comfortably in a society of merchants and philanthropists who formed the backbone of Saint Louis's social progress and of the Ethical Culture Society, a quasi-religious society, which in New York offered Jews a way of being Unitarian, but in Saint Louis, Cincinnati, and elsewhere possessed a truly interdenominational membership. My grandmother Lottie was talkative, red-headed, bowlegged, lopsided, humorous, and delightful. She was as headstrong as the procession of women who had formed her character. English was her first language and German her second. She had taught kindergarten, been active in Ethical Culture, was genteel to the point of imperiousness, and didn't have much real use for men. Her husband, Joe Weiner, a prematurely bald, clearfaced short man with a toothbrush moustache and a small wen on his cheek which he used to call his "lentil," was gentleness and forbearance itself with his bossy little wife, and he kept his temper, though sometimes with difficulty, by not saying much. After their marriage he kept industriously busy with his cotton business on lower Broadway, helped numerous relatives to come to America, and went off by himself to Temple Emanu-El. My grandmother bred true to her family pattern by producing two daughters, seven years apart.

My mother, Natalie Eva Weiner, was born in 1899. She inherited her mother's reddish hair and obstinacy, rather than her father's stolidity and phlegm. Her childhood was spent in apartments on the Upper West Side of Manhattan, and in Woodmere. She attended camps in Maine every summer and, after graduating from the Ethical Culture School, entered Barnard College in 1919. In the summers after the war she traveled several times to Europe and visited her father's relatives in Vienna and Trenčín. She grew up beautiful, intelligent, and willful. The boys she met at Columbia, around New York, at the Plaza tea dances, were few of them determined enough to handle her. For a year or so in her early twenties she had a love affair with a married man, a well-known playwright whose hundreds of love letters to her betrayed a sentimentality as tacky as the realism of his plays. Although she was strong enough to manage him (and in fact seems to have treated him very firmly indeed), the exertion of carrying on a hidden liaison brought on chronic colitis and persuaded her to seek psychotherapeutic help. When it was over, her father took her on the traditional long trip to Europe to recover. It was at the end of this journey, when she stopped in England to attend the Fabian Society School and visit friends in London, that she met my father.

They were a strong-willed and passionate pair, impulsive in bestowing affection, but proud and stiff in defense of their individual dignity. The bond between them, warmed by music and poetry, grew rigid and cold when it encountered physical sexuality. My mother's distrust of men, learned at her mother's knee, had been twisted into impatience by her succession of weak chivalrous New Yorkers, trained into wariness by the playwright, and crystallized by feminism. My father's childhood and youth, distorted by the absence of a father and by a poverty as formative as my mother's affluence, had endowed him with a romantic but overcharged attraction toward women, combined with a dark unquenchable suspicion that women would not keep their promises. My mother was the first girl in generations of her family to marry a gentile, a gentile who was not even a businessman. My father had no means of allaying the Weiners' qualms about a foreigner who spoke no German, an Englishman, a poet. Yet since he had never known any family except for his mother (his sister had been brought up mostly by an aunt), he embraced Natalie's family with unusual warmth. In time they accepted him even though he was more foreign to them, with his curly waving hair and his pipe and tweeds, than any Ruthenian.

The ostensible causes of quarrels do not vary greatly from family to family: money, relatives, insecurity, dependence, and independence—in this sense all *un*happy families are alike. Nobody could have predicted why these perennial causes should, in my family, have resulted in foaming, shrieking, door-slamming, table-pounding altercations. All my parents' gaiety, their outgoingness and their capacity for easy friendship, their resources of love and intensity that my sister and I have held as the bulwark of our lives for over forty years—none of these could avail against the tides of quarreling that they drowned in as helplessly as sex.

When the marriage was young, the quarrels came and went as quickly as thundershowers; but later, as my father found it increasingly difficult to write poetry and my mother began to spend more time outside the house on committee and political work, the quarrels began to hang over us all like monsoons. Money had always been a sensitive point. When Teddie arrived in America in 1925 he was deeply in debt, and although he worked furiously to pay off his English creditors, he did not completely clear the slate until my mother gave him enough to wipe the score out. It was a generous gesture, for which he was always grateful, but it had its corrosive aspect too. Teddie could never forget the days when his mother, alone in the north of England, with her two small children, had to wait every week for the money that, as often as not, "Uncle Ted" could not or would not pay. The memory of debt was always a shame to him, and all his life long he kept records upon records, all aligned in double entries in his exquisite bookkeeper's handwriting, out of anxiety lest the money somehow run out again.

He was not unrealistic. The salary of a full professor at the University of Colorado in the 1930s was about $4,000. My parents supplemented it by their management each summer of the Writers' Conference in the Rocky Mountains, which brought in an additional $1,500. In medical or other emergencies, or when it came time to buy a house, or when Beatrice could no longer be afforded, the Weiners might furnish additional money. My father's pride suffered from the help, welcome though it was, mainly because the family could not but regard his line of work as both unprofitable and incomprehensible.

The earliest quarrels I remember all had to do with money—with a check my mother had forgotten to enter, with some slipshod bit of housekeeping extravagance. The thunderstorms brewed up at the slightest drop of temperature, with or without pretext, but they always seemed to break over the dinner table, perhaps because of the drinking my father did beforehand. Dinnertime became the hour of anxiety, and in Colorado my sister and I preferred to eat in the kitchen with Beatrice. My mother, however, insisted that we should all dine together for the sake of family solidarity, so we sat at the big table by the windows that looked out into the lower branches of the apple trees, cringing when the quarrels broke over our heads. If one of us happened to spill a glass of milk or forget to put our knife and fork together when we were finished, or drink soup out of the point of the spoon instead of the side, there would be thunder from my father and answering lightning from my mother. Lesley developed a spastic intestinal condition out of fear of mealtimes.

My slippery ways served me pretty well: I kept on appealing to my father out of strength and my mother out of weakness. More and more as I climbed through school I rode under my father's literary colors, while my sister took a quirky but far less imitative approach to learning, preferring to choose a wrong road for herself rather than take directions from anyone else. She wrote poems and plays as well as *Davison Doings,* she organized what she called "fun classes" for groups of younger children, she drew and printed and kept up a steady output of verbal pitter-patter, while I read and daydreamed and ran about after the other boys. Over the dinner table, however, the oedipal order of battle was drawn. Both my sister and I tended to side with my mother in the quarrels, for she was less noisy and seemed to have more reason on her side. Her irritants and instigations, her sexual signals, were too subtle for children to understand.

As time went on, however, my sister and I began to follow divergent courses. When I was about ten my health, which had been so tenuous in my early childhood, began to strengthen. Colorado had been good for me. But at the same age my sister's teeth began to give trouble, and she became overweight, and she kept falling down and bruising knees and breaking arms. As I grew into my strength, living in the two worlds of books and exercise, my sister seemed to seek out lacerations, illness, and trouble, and my mother crowded to protect her. It was an inevitable pity that she chose to defend the child against my father, electing him as the most dangerous threat. My sister could be an infuriating girl, and my father didn't suffer irritants gladly; but her imagination was sublime. Teddie oscillated between outrage at her stubbornness and enchantment with her talents. My mother, in a performance designed I fear mostly for Teddie's eyes, hovered around my sister like a broody hen. When necessary she would interpose herself between Lesley and my father's wrath; but on some occasions it was Lesley who was volunteered as the stalking-horse for the perennial and gradually intensifying wrangle between man and wife. What had begun as a courtship display had now hardened into a private and dangerous Peloponnesian War.

How my sister divined the meaning of all this, I have never inquired; but like any perceptive child she must have used the strife for what she conceived to be her own purposes. Before many years had passed she had learned how to provoke incidents quickly enough if they did not provoke themselves. It all got worse when we had to leave Boulder. In 1943, when I was fifteen and my sister thirteen, my father was called to Washington, first as a civilian and later as a major in the Army. That summer we stored the books and furniture and followed him, leaving home behind us, traversing the continent yet again. The journey in our old Oldsmobile took ten days at the thirty-five-mile-per-hour speed limit imposed by wartime regulations. My mother did all the driving. We arrived in Washington weary and confused, only a few days before I was due to return by train to Colorado for boarding school. The family would inhabit a series of cramped furnished dwellings in Washington for the next three years. There, where my mother soon took a war job in the Office of War Information, I lost any sense of home as a physical surrounding. Our house was only the place where my family lived, where my models for life awaited me, where love tugged me and anger churned me up, but it was home no longer once we left Boulder behind.

When I returned to Washington during school vacation, the dinner hours had become almost intolerable in their bathos and acrimony. By 1944, when my mother and father were both working full tilt six days a week, and I too had taken a job as a page in the U.S. Senate, and my sister sat at home practicing the saxophone and playing Bing Crosby records, four exhausted and nerve-wracked people gathered every evening around the constricted arena of a dining table, and every night precipitated an explosion. Everyone else talked so much that I did not dare to. One night as I sat listening to the ranting and accusations, to the deep rage of my father's voice, to the high defensive righteousness of my mother's, to the pigheaded adolescent intractability of my sister's, I made then and there the first fully calculated decision of my life: never again would I allow any of these three to grapple my emotions for any purpose. I would simply lock up these emotions within myself, would compose myself into a cool statue, and take on the role of bland neutrality in these unceasing family rows. I was slippery enough to succeed in my aim, but I paid the price in later years.

Not long after this decision I came downstairs after a post-prandial altercation when my father had huffed out of the house and my mother was gloomily washing the dishes, and found spread on the cleared-off dining room table a long typed memorandum from him to her, accusing her of lack of consideration and amity in their sexual life. It took me two paragraphs before I understood what the document was about, and I flushed with horror and embarrassment. I quickly replaced it in its envelope and put the envelope on my mother's little maple desk in a back alcove behind the dining room. To be dragged into this too! It was intolerable. Now I resolved to sever myself from the family as quickly and completely as I possibly could, to spend as much time away from "home" as I could manage, at boarding school, at college, later on and forever. The gravity of my love for my parents and my sister was made too poignant for me by their constantly wounding and tearing at one another, and I didn't know how to fight back.

So it was that, instead of mounting a normal adolescent rebellion against my parents on a common home ground, and pitting my own newly discovered values against theirs for testing, I simply ran away from the fray, taking with me their life styles and beliefs for my own use in the outside world. From sixteen on I employed the masks of my parents' generation in a life at school and work where I could forget the ensanguined rooms of home, where I could pretend to be master of my emotions by denying them. My sister, for whom escape was not yet possible, stayed on and fought her own fight. I felt myself too weak to follow suit.

But one does not run away from such a battle without leaving hostages, and I was simply postponing the day. I would not achieve genuine independence from my parents till I was thirty. Wherever I went I was drawn to my family as onlooker rather than participant, with the terrible fascination of a man witnessing a murder in his dreams, or with the avidity of the Peeping Tom. I could not join the donnybrook, but I could not avert my eyes from it. It was only an illusion that I had made myself immune to the emotions that my parents' strife aroused, and in the attempt I risked making myself immune to emotion altogether. Only on my periodic visits to the bosom of my family could I be sure of either feeling love or suffering pain.

4.

Still, when I returned to boarding school on the Colorado plains, I was better able to distinguish my parents as individuals, apart from the miasma of emotion that surrounded them when we were together. In Colorado, at a distance, I could weigh and test them, look at them through eyes that were beginning to be trained, with the adversary sharpness that adolescence brings with it. My father came to the end of the war in a state of near-exhaustion, but he stayed on in the Army for some months to finish his military task: the reeducation and retraining of liberal German prisoners of war to fit them for positions in a putative postwar German democracy. The undertaking was as useful as Army work could ever be, but its administration fell under the bludgeon of military inertia. The plans made for the prisoners were one thing; carrying them out under the military government was another. Hundreds of key Germans, ready and willing to take up positions in government, in the press and communications, arrived home to find that their instructions had been forever mislaid in the tangle of the Occupation bureaucracy. Nothing of the plan that had cost millions and exhausted my father and his staff was ever carried out. Only years later, when the history of postwar German literature would come to be written, would it be revealed that the "Gruppe 47," including such writers as Hans Werner Richter and Alfred Andersch, had taken its beginnings from one of my father's POW camps, Fort Getty, Rhode Island. Richter, moreover, translated some of my father's poems into German.

Our Colorado years had been good for the family as a whole, but they had offered little to nourish my mother's feminist spirit. Also, she aspired to some form of distinction that would impress them back in New York, the only place that really counted, and her considerable ambitions for us were cribbed by Boulder's possibilities. In 1939, contrary to all reason, she had persisted in the belief and hope that Teddie would be made president of the University of Colorado on the retirement of George Norlin, the austere and kindly classical scholar who had guided the university for twenty years and who had brought my father to Colorado in the first place. Why she imagined that an English poet (my father was not yet a naturalized U.S. citizen) without full academic credentials, married to a Jewish wife and without any political or social attachment to Colorado or the West, might be chosen president of the state university in 1939 can only be explained as a New Yorker's *folie de grandeur*. Teddie knew better, perhaps.

When we left Boulder it was, I imagine, to my mother's relief. In Washington she quickly built a professional life for herself at the Office of War Information, while my father traveled widely among the POW camps and I was away at school. She shopped and kept house for herself and Lesley and often for a lodger or two as well, but went off to her office in the Social Security Building every morning. It was an exhausting life, but it counted as her own.

The war ended, but my father did not press for a discharge. While he stayed on in Washington to finish up the repatriation of the prisoners, my mother took on a new job collecting cattle and beasts of burden for the ravaged populations of eastern Europe. When my father's Army service finally came to an end, my parents had decisions to make: no matter how interesting my mother found Washington, there was no long-term employment there for my father. Colorado wanted him back, but that consideration was rejected. He declined the presidency of the University of Seoul in Korea. A teaching job was the thing, preferably something near New York, so that my mother could continue her career; but by this time it was the summer of 1946, everyone else had come home from the war, and the desirable jobs were all gone. My father, without a Ph.D., was no conventional scholar, no matter how brilliant a teacher or notable a poet, and both his scholarship and his poetry had fallen into arrears. The only new specialty he had to offer was administration, the evidence of having planned an education for half a million prisoners.

In the autumn of 1946, tired and dispirited, he settled for a job that combined teaching and administration, the position of dean at Washington and Jefferson, a small liberal arts college in western Pennsylvania. During his first year there he lived in a furnished room, and traveled back and forth two hundred miles to our Washington, D.C., house by bus on weekends while my mother concluded her job of war relief. By this time I had entered Harvard, and Lesley was attending a nearby boarding school, the Cambridge School of Weston, Massachusetts. It was a trying period, made no less confusing by the presence of two Washingtons and two Cambridges in the family vocabulary, and of two diverging professional lives as well as two tangents of education.

By 1947 my mother with some reluctance gave up UNRRA in order to fix a home base for us in Washington, Pennsylvania. The family books and furniture were finally extricated from storage in Colorado and shoehorned into a small white frame house on a side street under the Pennsylvania elms. Behind it lay a generous plot of land, perhaps half an acre, where my father could dig himself a new vegetable garden. For my mother there was little to do but act the housekeeper and hostess.

Here we all tried to regroup, but after the interruption of the war, like other families, we found that the rules had changed. My father, presiding in the dean's office over the administration of curricula and discipline, labor he had to force himself to do, was unable to find his way back to poetry, too hurried to do much of the teaching he was a past master of. Permanently tired and congenitally disappointed, he began to drink more steadily than before. When my mother arrived with her household effects, still chafing at the necessity to make a burnt offering of her new career, he took to guilty drinking and she, justified by her sacrifice, could not bring herself to take seriously the everyday imbroglios of faculty intrigue.

Lesley and I had left Colorado far behind us and now, like most adolescents, looked to the cities for adventure and the thrill of danger that went with discovery. When we made the expected trips home for college vacations, we found Washington, Pennsylvania, drearily dull: we had outgrown college towns, and the one we called "Washpa" offered neither the beauty nor the peace of Boulder. Our dislike of the latest turn in our family's affairs enabled us, for the first time in years, to draw together in order to pull away from our parents. We formed an unholy adolescent alliance of song and sarcasm. Lesley was learning the guitar and hundreds of folk songs. She would soon begin to write satirical songs of her own. She and I began to perform together, and we took to singing for our parents' friends, yielding the impression, not altogether false, of a wholesome and devoted family group. Yet our singing, our alliance in despite of the older generation, was our way of getting a word in edgewise through the spaces between our parents' endless and baleful wrangling. Music in our family was the food of love, and if our folk singing concealed a panicky childhood anxiety for ourselves and a contempt for our parents' disquiet, no one could possibly construe it as part of the war between the generations. When my sister grasped her guitar and ran her fingers over the strings between songs, my parents made requests, but she always played whatever song she wanted to and not what they requested. The guitar was her skeleton key to independence. I had yet to find my own.

As my parents ceased to be able to furnish me a dependably secure cradle, I began to despise them for that failure. Perhaps I would have despised them—or myself—equally if they had succeeded. Like many dependent children, I resented their incapacity to detect those moments when I wanted comfort. I was furious that they should be distracted by their own concerns. I scorned their irrational streaks, their instability. No critics can be so excoriating or so selfish as the young, whether they speak their criticism or fabricate a mask of indifference, as I did. We intermittently hate our parents during the critical period of adolescence because, no matter how we love them, they have failed us. We cannot forgive them if they make us walk out into the cold, into exile, just as we can never forgive them if they do not.

Obedient to my vow over the Washington dinner table during the war, I kept away from home as much as I could contrive or afford. Many people at eighteen or nineteen find themselves a substitute home, and mine for a while was my grandmother Weiner's apartment in New York. There I could count on a welcome whenever I turned up, a love unimpeded by the rivalry between generations, a *pied-à-terre* in the heart of the city where I could meet my friends, go to the theatre, restaurants, and the Great World on my own terms, yet have Granny waiting at home to keep me from feeling lonely.

My grandmother was at this time in her middle seventies, a

bowlegged, pince-nezed, misshapen little hellion with an impish sense of humor lurking beneath her unblushing complacency over her daughters and grandchildren. When I was a freshman at college my grandfather died, and we were encouraged to visit my grandmother often in the first loneliness of her widowhood. I often took the train from Washington or Boston, dragged my suitcase uptown on the subway, blew into Granny's apartment for a bite of dinner in the hotel restaurant, jollied her over the pot roast and creamed spinach, and set off on my rambles in the big town. Her love was blind but not deaf. Nothing could have suited me better. When, years later, I first read Proust, I recognized in Marcel's summers at Balbec with his grandmother many of the pleasures that had been mine—a comfortable place to rest, a warm and devoted affection, the satisfaction of my desires without more than the most elementary demands on my own attention. Pleasures like these were no longer to be found at my parents' home, where songs of complicity and snarls of rage alternated in Dionysiac succession. I wanted soothing and spoiling. I wanted nothing asked of me.

My grandmother lived in a three-room furnished flat in the Bradford, then a moderately luxurious residential hotel on Seventieth Street west of Broadway. The smell I encountered the moment I stepped off the elevator at the tenth floor included the unmistakable odors of furniture polish, carpet sweepers, and Lysol, mixed with some sort of exhalation from the leaded paint that glutted the walls. Entering the door of my grandmother's apartment after a fervent exchange of hugs, I passed the kitchenette alcove into a parlor with a pleasant southerly view over what is now Lincoln Center. Plaster cornices blurred the angles of the walls. The furniture ran to embroidered satin and mahogany, day beds, sofas, three-legged tables; the lamps to silk shades with fringes. Prints hung on the walls: the city gates at Rothenburg, Napoleon with his hand in his waistcoat, Lincoln ditto, the Marienkirche at Munich, the castle at Chillon. On the tables stood framed photographs of my grandmother's family past and present: the Herzogs, the Cullmanns, the Davisons, the Andrews; and a few of my grandfather's family, the Weiners.

I slept in a spare parlor-bedroom on the left. Here were more photographs of my grandparents on their frequent European travels before the war, of my uncle and aunt Andrews on their honeymoon at Atlantic City, of my mother and father on their wedding day in a nearby New York hotel, and of us grandchildren posing for the camera beside dogs and toys and carts and boxes. Against one wall stood a glassed-in bookcase containing novels by Hervey Allen and Konrad Bercovici, Santayana's *The Last Puritan,* and my father's pink-jacketed *Collected Poems,* Harper & Brothers, 1940. There was plenty of hotel stationery on a small desk. The bathrooms gleamed with monumental fixtures, porcelain faucet handles, powerful hydraulic toilets with little shaggy jackets on their lids, medicine closets full of Pears soap, antacid powders, and all sorts of pills and tonics compounded at a doctor's orders, many still left from my dead grandfather's time. The bureaus had glass tops. Sometimes I ate dinner with my grandmother in the hotel dining room— shrimp and herring, roast beef and lamb chops, creamed greens and buttered beets, ice cream and apple pie, served by waiters called Otto or Franz with German or Czech accents. When I could, I went to dine by myself at the Fleur-de-Lys, my first French restaurant, where I could pay ninety-nine cents to feel worldly on *tête de veau vinaigrette, cervelles beurre noire,* or *boeuf à la bourguignonne* and a glass of wine. The corner of Seventy-second Street and Broadway was a center of a sort of life that no longer takes place there in the era of *Mr. Sammler's Planet:* florists' shops and chophouses, hotels that were really hotels, men sitting on benches reading foreign-language newspapers.

My grandmother's little apartment was the place where for several years I felt most at home. When I returned at night after a play or a visit, Granny was always in, awake or snoring in the other bedroom. We might have a glass of milk together, and in the morning she would boil me an egg in her kitchenette and babble about her slights and outrages and how hard poor Aunt Isabel's life was in her Park Avenue apartment with only one maid. I could listen to her with half an ear, tease her and flirt with her, read the paper, and be on my way. It seemed—no, it was—home for me then. When I graduated from boarding school in 1945 I listed it in the yearbook as my permanent home address, to my parents' indignation, even though I knew it was only an address.

5.

The shudder with which I turned my back on my parents' troubles in my late teens and early twenties was so automatic that I find it hard to call to mind how distressed their unhappiness made me then. Nor can I recall how my indifference affected them. We cannot bear, while we are still children, to think of our parents as unhappy. The child's world is so narrow and self-centered that he can understand only the pains and terrors that plague *him,* or the contemporaries in whom he sees *himself* reflected. That his parents, in spite of all his love for them, should actually suffer pain and grief confounds him. Later, as the adult begins to emerge from the child, he develops greater skill in detecting fear, weariness, frustration in his parents. As he discovers their flaws in the growing light and fading warmth of adolescence, he marks down each flaw as a weakness. If his parents cannot be happy, it is because they haven't *tried*. If hostile forces warp their lives, his parents are weak and contemptible for not having overcome. He does not hesitate to indict them, out of his bright new certainty, on charges of corruption or failure.

Like most boys of seventeen and eighteen, I found it fascinating to judge and test my parents' lives. What had they been like at *my* age? Now for the first time I read my father's poems, seeking clues to the secrets of his youth. With my mother the reconnaissance took a rather different form—a new relationship based on an old foundation. We began to evolve a teasing yet flirtatious alliance, using lessons I had learned from girls and polished up on my susceptible grandmother. With my mother the teasings were sometimes pointed enough to be actually cruel, just as my flirtation with her had a more serious purpose than it did with others.

On my visits home to Pennsylvania or, several years later, to New York, I could hardly wait until my father left the house for his office and I could sit with my mother over the breakfast table and talk—talk about myself, of course, *my* friends, *my* girls, *my* achievements at school or college or elsewhere. I listened with outward interest to her accountings of her time, her news of work at her office or volunteer job of the moment, of her generous political concerns. She believed in social service, in liberal politics, in reform. In Pennsylvania she worked hard in the war against air pollution (the windows of houses became etched by the noxious air every few years) . Later, after my parents returned to New York for good in 1950, she would become active in Americans for

Democratic Action, in Democratic party reform under the leadership of Eleanor Roosevelt and Herbert Lehman in the long but ultimately successful campaign to break the power of Tammany Hall. But I listened to her chronicles with a secret impatience, as one who gives up hostages in order to negotiate, inwardly hoping that after the next interruption of the telephone, I could manipulate the conversation back to where it belonged and talk about myself.

So the mornings lengthened, the breakfast dishes still unwashed, my mother still in her dressing gown, her heavy breasts loosening it as often as she tugged it tight again, her hair, not so red as it had been, disheveled. The telephone would ring and my mother would answer, talking, laughing, murmuring, but when it was over she would return to me, and *listen*. A confession of troubles could still hold her attention better than a procession of triumphs; a real or pretended illness never failed, even then, to draw her to my side. Only mothers, perhaps, have the depth and patience, the nursing instinct, that will let them listen totally—mothers, or wives who are mothers to their husbands. Perhaps it is the memory of this devoted listening that identifies for us that magic moment when we first fall in love and realize, senses fully alerted by desire, that our lovers are listening, with that familiar intensity and compassion, to *us*.

In the evenings of my visits home I would get my mother to make music with me. Sometimes my father sang with her the songs they knew, but now I edged her into trying new things, more Schumann, Elizabethan lute songs, Fauré chansons, as well as the ones I had learned with Mrs. Kempner years before. As time went by, it was more often my father, drink in hand and blank-faced, who sat listening while my mother and I made music together, music he would not learn and would not sing, though his was the better voice.

6.

I have already spoken of my father's voice, that remarkable instrument. The possessor of such an asset is not likely to be encouraged by the world to listen well. It was up to me to do the listening. By the time I was in college the closest years of our relationship were already behind us, immured in those summer evenings in Colorado when he would sit in the dusk on our broad porch and smoke his pipe and sip his ever-present drink and watch the leaves move in the boughs of the trees of his garden—the apple, the silver spruce, the cotton-wood, the mountain ash, which he insisted on calling a "rowan." Fifteen years after emigrating, he retained an English accent with hardly a trace of the New World in it, an accent he would never lose. The intonations of his voice and the cadences of his speech had been formed by the Book of Common Prayer, the King James Bible, and the lyric tradition of English poetry.

As a child in the north of England, my father commanded, as he was fond of telling me, the highest and purest boy soprano in Yorkshire. He had dreamed for a while, after it changed to tenor, of an operatic career, which never materialized. He had a singing range of three octaves, and until a mysterious strangling cough hoarsened him in his fifties, an uncanny range of tone. His voice and his love for the English language made him an irresistible lecturer and a mesmeric reciter of poetry. He could rattle windows with a shout, chill the blood with the modulations of his voice, make himself heard at the back of any hall in a whisper. I have never heard his equal in the reading of English poetry aloud, except for Dylan Thomas, whom, curiously, he resembled, with his small bones, potbelly, squint eyes, and curly hair.

Our years in Boulder, during my father's thirties, were the most tranquil of his life. As he sat on the covered porch, lines and stanzas of poetry would drift through his mind, passages from novels, memories from his past. I often came out to sit by him in the cool dusk. Sometimes we sat silently together. Whatever he spoke about, poetry fell from the air. His memory was prodigious, and his talk was streaked with the colors of rhyme and rhythm. Much of his rambling discourse on the porch could be classified as Advice for the Conduct of Life, when his opinions took on a sententious ring, as though the mantle of fatherhood didn't quite fit. He was given to pomposity and even such unforgettably worthless nonsense as: "Hairy men tend to stink when they sweat" (despite his sounding the tocsin, I have never found this to be true), or: "Beware of jealousy, not only in yourself but in others. The curse of my life has been other men's jealousy of me." He also spoke of literature and of poets, always with a reverence for the language that had rescued him from obscurity and poverty when he was a young man. His talk then flared with streamers, all new to me, lightening the summer darkness:

> How with this rage shall beauty hold a plea
> Whose action is no stronger than a flower?

> The bearer of evil tidings
> When he was halfway there
> Remembered that evil tidings
> Were a dangerous thing to bear. . . .

Leave the bottle on the chimleypiece, and don't ask me to take none, but let me put my lips to it when I am so dispoged.

"Ah, if there shall ever arise a nation whose people have forgotten poetry or whose poets have forgotten the people, though they send their ships round Taprobane and their armies across the hills of Hindostan . . . what of them?" "They will be a dark patch upon the earth."

That thou art my son I have partly thy mother's word, partly mine own opinion, but chiefly a villainous trick of thine eye and a foolish hanging of thy nether lip that doth warrant me.

> Be not afeard. The isle is full of noises,
> Sounds, and sweet airs, that give delight and hurt not.

> The little dogs and all,
> Tray, Blanch, and Sweetheart, see, they bark at me.

> But twice unhappier is he, I lairn,
> That feidis in his heart a mad desire,
> And follows on a woman throw the fire,
> Led by a blind and teachit by a bairn.

My father's natural sententiousness was shot through with such music. It transmuted his most oppressive pronouncements, softened the discomfort of his self-pity, allayed the intractability of his life, and bred an acolyte in his son. He was a strange man. I am sure I never understood him as well as he did me, yet his words and his voice, till the day of his death, held a special resonance in my mind. Scorn his views or pity his cautionary maxims as I might, I could never cease to revere him for the poetry that clothed his utterance like no one else's, the sounds and syllables of English that pealed from him like bells.

The official account of his early life held that his father had died when Teddie was a child of four. When I turned eighteen Teddie took me to dinner at the elegant old Lafayette Hotel in New York. After a chop and a bottle of claret, while we sat over cigars and port at one of the marble-topped tables, he told me for the first time the truth about the circumstances of his childhood. There was something in the

expression of his face and the unaccustomed hush of his voice
that made me realize I was being told not only a secret but a
legend.

My grandmother, his mother, had gone as a governess to a
house in the north of England when she was a young woman
in the 1890s. She fell in love with the master of the house,
and in due course bore him two children—my father in 1898
and his sister four years later. Not until fifteen years after
that did my grandfather's wife die, and only then, with some
reluctance, did he marry my grandmother.

It was a strangely English, a peculiarly Edwardian saga. At
the age of twelve Teddie had to leave school and take jobs in
factories, offices, a music hall, because his father could not or
would not support the second household. And—Teddie pronounced this with terrible emphasis over the table at the
Lafayette—he had always hated his father; they had always
quarreled; his father *drank*. My grandmother, innocent and
trusting, had expected her man to take care of her, and she
adored him despite everything till the end of her life; but it
was Teddie whose youth and strength had been sacrificed to
making up the nonfeasances of my grandfather.

There was a pause. "What was his name?" I asked.

"Shields," my father said, "Edward Shields."

"Then why isn't our name Shields?"

"Our name is *Davison*," he replied, and said nothing more.

It was a startling though hardly a shocking story, but the
manner of its telling was strange, uncharacteristic, almost
ritualized. Years later, after my father's death, I talked to one
of his early loves, whom at the height of their friendship he
had taken out to dinner and told the same story.

"It was curious," she said. "He seemed to regard his illegitimacy as more of a stigma than I did, or than any of my
friends would have. That was 1924, but illegitimacy was not

so *very* unusual. I could not help feeling at the time as though your father was using it as, what do you say, an alibi?"

Teddie seldom spoke again to me of his revelation except in dark references to "my father" and "my childhood," though he often spoke of his mother. From time to time he did talk of writing reminiscences of his early years, but, though he made a try at a beginning at least as early as 1931, he never prospered in the attempt until just before his death in 1970, when he composed the fragment which follows:

MY EARLY CHILDHOOD

by Edward Davison

I was born in Scotland, at Glasgow, on July 28, 1898, the son of Evelyn Mary Davison. Years later, when I first saw my birth certificate, it showed only a blank space in the panel provided for my father's name. I remember nothing of Glasgow until I stayed there overnight in 1922 on my way to Loch Lomond. By that time my parents had been married for five years and I was a new-fledged Bachelor of Arts and still a resident student at St. John's College, Cambridge.

Memories of my early infancy are sparse and indistinctly set in the seaside town of South Shields. There on the Durham side of the River Tyne I found myself put out to nurse with Mrs. Rush, a stoutish middle-aged widow, and her daughter Emma, plain, good-hearted, respectable Tyneside folk. They must have taken some kind of pride in their charge, enough it seems for Mrs. Rush to have paid out of her own pocket for an over-posed photograph of herself (spectacled and dignified in a black bonnet and gown, both with sequins) and me, aged three, wide-eyed and wearing a white straw hat and sailor suit. I still have that picture and can clearly recall the taking of it because the proceedings were disappointingly flawed by my not being enough alert to spot the "little bird" that was alleged to have flown out of the camera at the crucial moment. Little bird, thou never wert! My mother frequently descended upon us bearing gifts and fragrance from some rarer world and those visits were to me times of excited delight. At a much too tender age I was admitted to the infants' class at the nearby Laygate Lane School, undoubtedly a false start on the educational track. One clear recollection remains. Some woman teacher for I know not what misdeed of mine gave me a smacking on my bare behind. This was my first lesson in public humiliation and I wept, not for the pain but for the exposure and the shame. As soon as my mother heard of this indignity she reprimanded the authorities at the school and banished it forever from her small son.

Soon afterwards, when I had just turned four, she came to take me away to Yorkshire. By that time there were three of us. The newcomer, my sister Amy, was a grave and sturdy brown-eyed baby whose birth certificate when I came upon it in after years displayed another blank space, the sinister counterpart of my own. I have fragmentary recollections of a train journey and of our settling down somewhere on the outskirts of Leeds in a terrace of little brick houses, all neat and new and exactly alike. Uncle Ted had joined us probably at Newcastle where we changed trains. This was my first acquaintance with him, or, for that matter, with any grown-up of my own sex. After the unpacking he disappeared as strangely as he had arrived, leaving only the faintest impression on my mind, for I was incurious about everything save my mother and the excitement of coming to live in a new place. So in the ripening autumn of 1902 my life began to take shape as it slipped unaware into the opening of the new century.

We had occasional visitors in Leeds. One of them, Aunt Olive, the younger of my mother's two sisters, would not believe as I did that a black bear lived at large in our attic after dark. She tried vainly to reason away my dread of it, but nothing could persuade me to leave the firelit sitting room and climb the stairs to put the matter to the proof. After some days when she and mother ceased to tease me, the bear and my fears soon melted away. Except for this I recall no misgivings about the dark. One day Aunt Olive took me to the Leeds Hippodrome to see a live panorama. In one scene Napoleon (it must have been) surprised a sentry asleep at his post in the midst of a snowstorm and sentenced him to be shot. I was horrified by the execution and for days afterwards miserably distressed for the poor sentry. The stone lions outside one of the public buildings in Leeds fascinated me. They were replicas, I now believe, of Landseer's sculptures in Trafalgar Square. But neither the London lions nor those that stand guard before the Public Library in New York ever impressed me as much as the lions of Leeds. Yet another visitor, Aunt Hilda, took us to the gardens of a mansion near the city to see a parade of peacocks, their fantails disspread flaunting purple and green, brilliantly ablaze in the afternoon sunlight, altogether a flashing display. I remember another time when we were part of a crowd that had overflowed the seating at a summer band concert. The park attendants ordered us off the grass and I felt a wave of hot indignation as we were chivvied willy-nilly out of the shade and away from the music. Also there was a day when I saw a pretty wax doll in a shop window and was overwhelmingly smitten with a desire to have it for my own. My mother and Aunt Olive however flatly and altogether unsympathetically refused to buy it for me, declaring that dolls were only for girls and that a big boy, like me, should be ashamed for wanting of all things a doll. Everybody would laugh at me. But I had fallen in love, helplessly and hopelessly, for the first time in my life and that bout of passion ended with a slapping. They were genuinely ashamed of me and I was put to bed filled with frustration and resentment.

But my most vivid and abiding memory of those days is of the afternoon when my mother, with the baby in her arms, left the house to call on some neighbor and was caught by a violent thunderstorm. A few weeks earlier, surprised by a similar disturbance, I had watched her draw the window blinds and curtains, and screen the mirror under a towel, and then with her fingers closed over her ears crouch into a clothes closet seeking as it were a further fold of protection against the frightening din. I had not been in the least infected by her panic. In truth I felt scornful of it, rather ashamed that my own beloved mother could behave like that. In later years I came to realize that she regarded herself as a sinful woman who might well be marked down for punishment by the wrath of an offended God. But now when I had a whole raging storm to myself and no one to hamper me I was exalted rather than afraid. Planted by the street door, barely beyond reach of the downpour though spattered by the edges of its spray, while the thunder cracked closer and louder overhead, I was beginning to rejoice timidly on the peak of my own bravado: except that my mother was out there in the storm and I should be doing something to help her. But what? Knowing that she must be very frightened, not only for herself and the baby but also for me alone at home, I thought of sallying out along the soaking terrace in search of her. But suppose in my absence she should come back to find the house empty and me missing? This was a dilemma. Soon I was feeling as sorry for myself as I was for her. So I watched and waited by the door until the storm began to mutter itself away. Meanwhile I became conscious of a peculiar odor on the air, acrid and faintly sickening. Could it have something to do with the now dwindling storm? The rain had stopped, the clouds were beginning to break, and a first shaft of sunlight beamed its way through them while the unfamiliar odor became more insistently pungent and distasteful until, at last, there was my mother waving to me from along the terrace and then all three of us were together again, sound and secure at home. Of course she had been worried about me. I was affectionately scolded for having waited at the open door in peril of the storm; something I must never *never* do again. Now we would have tea and afterwards she would read me a story. The queer smell she casually dismissed as "only something cooking next door." But the impression of that smell lingered on in my olfactory memory for years afterwards to be vividly resuscitated whenever I was overtaken by a thunderstorm. Nearly always at the onset I would find myself mysteriously expectant, my nostrils alert for the first thrust of the sharp, strange, unforgotten odor. In spite of all my anticipations it never once came. Lightning and thunder were potent to revivify my memory of it; but the odor itself when I happened upon it would snatch me instantly away from wherever in time or space I chanced at the moment to be and set me back in time inside the consciousness of a four-year-old boy, alone and anxious about his mother. I would be rapt again in the atmosphere and circumstances of the original storm. Several times, accidentally but always in fair weather, I was to re-encounter the actual smell, once (pungent and unmistakable) in a street on Brooklyn Heights where it floated up from an open half-basement window; and again, years later, in France, in the fumes of a shabby restaurant near St. Cloud. The identification and denouement did not occur until I was a man of forty when in the kitchen of my own house a baking pie overflowed and the spilling juice of ripe plums seethed and scorched on the hot metal of the oven. And so the ghost of that odor was finally laid.

Such were the trivial morsels of experience that fastened themselves on my memory as a very young child. Consciousness, significance have to begin somewhere. These were their small awakenings in me.

The stay at Leeds cannot have lasted for more than a few months. I have no recollection of a return journey, but some time before the midsummer of 1903 we were back again in South Shields, or rather in that least salubrious part of it known to the world of seamen and shipping as Tyne Dock. Porchester Street was dreary and short, almost a cul-de-sac, shut off for most purposes by a high railway embankment at one end. Two identical rows of brick dwellings, each row with its own paved walk, faced one another two stories high across the cobbled width of the street. There were tufts of grass sprouting green in the gutters and between the gray cobblestones. Clusters of chimney pots smoked on each ridge above the smooth slated rooves. Our be-it-ever-so-humble new home, number 17, was a ground floor unit. You entered the front door through a minute lobby, passed through a very small bedroom into a larger bed-sitting-room containing a fireplace with kettle hobs and, beyond this, a kind of kitchen or scullery where a sink and a single cold-water tap kept company with the smallest possible iron cook stove and oven. Coal was our sole fuel for heating and cooking. Coal gas piped into the house through a penny-in-the-slot meter could be used only for lighting. The stove, when it was fully fired, provided some scanty overflow of heat and the sitting room fireplace could warm at least one room. Nevertheless the house could be miserably bleak and chilly, especially on winter mornings. Hot water for every purpose had to be boiled in a kettle. The wash-boiler, a tublike caldron at the rear of the scullery where it was built in with its own private firebox, was a ravenous devourer of coal. The kitchen door opened on to a cement backyard that was partly enclosed by a brick wall. Two coal cabins and the outhouse (in Tyneside parlance "the nettie") abutted on the back lane. The yard and its conveniences were shared with our upstairs neighbors. The weekly rent for this dwelling and its primitive appurtenances was four shillings and threepence, which added up to about £11.0.0 a year, equal in American money at that time to $55. Gas and coal, of course, were extras. These quarters by the standards of that time were somewhat better than most. They were more or less typical of the mushroom housing that sprang up in most industrial towns in North England about the turn of the century to provide for the working class. Families who cared enough could keep them decent and clean. Poor as they were they did not rate as slums. Our street was tidy and unlittered. Each doorway had its own stone step and domestic ritual required the woman of the house to scrub and scour it almost every day. After its anointment with bathbrick, the whiteness of her doorstep was to nearly every housewife in Porchester Street the accepted badge and exterior certificate of her family's respectability. Also, sadly enough, it was all too often a symbolic denial of the very real poverty within, especially when the man of the house was un-employed or locked out or on strike. Most of the shady or really bad characters who lived on our street could be spotted by the dirtiness of their doorsteps. But even as a small boy I paradoxically realized that some of the whitest doorsteps on the street belonged to people who seemed to me harsh or mean. I made friends with Mr. Thomson, the bearded milkman whose pony trap clattered with a jingle of harness along the street to stop (with no need for a whoa to the pony) at each customer's door. He would ladle the milk out of his big can and pour into your own jug the imperial gill or half-pint of your order. (Milk soured easily over-night and there were no available means of refrigeration.) Some-times I managed to beg a scrap of stale bread or some carrot tops or even a lump of sugar for the pony. Mr. Thomson would doff his bowler hat to my mother, ring his hand-bell, and be off on his round. But he always had a jovial word for me and I some chatter for him. Later on I learned to keep watch for the postman. There were three deliveries each weekday. Once, perhaps, in a week there would be a letter for my mother, either from Aunt Hilda or Aunt Olive, or, less often, from Uncle Ted. His, when it came, usually by the last post on a Saturday evening after interminable waiting and anxiety on my mother's part, might enclose a postal order that could be cashed in time to buy immediate necessities like bread, butter, milk, potatoes, cabbage, tea, and the scrag end of a leg of mutton for Sunday's dinner. When there was no such letter and therefore no enclosure, the butcher, fortunately, al-lowed small purchases on temporary credit. So did Mrs. Bell, who sold sweets for children and various staple groceries in the only shop, almost next door to us, on Porchester Street. Although the rent began gradually to fall into arrears our landlord some-how suffered it without evicting us. These tolerances were un-doubtedly attributable to my mother's habitual bearing, her warmth and vivacity. She was not only young, very pretty and graceful, but unmistakably educated, well-informed, and remark-ably articulate. An aloofness of manner innocent of any condescension or superiority added a certain charm to those attributes and impressed most of the people she met. Many of the younger married women would come to her for advice about their babies, and their husbands took off their hats to her in the street.

This was not the world of my father's poetry, which he learned from the Book of Common Prayer, from the Everyman's Library, and from the advice and guidance of friends more than from any teachers, with the single exception of Arthur Quiller-Couch. Throughout the years in which he wrote, he would try, and fail, to come to grips with the wounds and angers of his actual life in his writings. A writer may traverse his apprentice period, and enter his years of promise, but until he has dealt, directly or indirectly, with the unique and ineluctable materials of his own life, he is unlikely ever to achieve maturity as a writer. So it was with my father. As we both grew older I urged him to write his story, and in this I was warmly seconded by friends like J. B. Priestley. The passage above is all he ever wrote of it. Till the age of forty he wrote lyric poetry, some of it beautiful, but little of it—with the notable exception of some of his best poems, like "In This Dark House" and "The Secret"—ever touched even indirectly on the grievance he bore all his days. His poetry was an exaltation rather than a fathoming.

7.

I emerged from adolescence ready to strike out on my own from the strangely altered, middle-aged lives of my parents; but there was not enough strength in me to break the bonds early. Some of the most precious ties would in fact be broken only by death. My last photograph of my mother, taken less than a year before she died at sixty, shows her in black, biting her lip in concentration at the piano, while I, thirty years old, stand behind her with hands folded in the singer's attitude, mouth piously agape with music. The picture shows that the singer is quite aware of his audience, quite conscious that the song is demanding.

My mother died clammy and deprived of all speech, her tongue gnarled and clumsied by the cancer that killed her. Twelve years later my father, half blind and his liver ruined by drink, within a month or two after having at last written the pages I have quoted, went down in a last delirium that was loud with fragments of whispered and chanted poetry that bobbed to the surface as he sank.

II

A Credit to the Family

Here in a strange town
I stand before a book
In a climate swollen with men
Who scuffle and leer outside
Across a street I can
Not cross, a lifetime wide.
For nearly twenty years
I shall not turn again
To hang around with the boys,
To lean and take a look,
To whistle at my fears.
I shall burrow among women.

P. D., "Rites of Passage: 1946"

1.

During the years of the war, while my family was being displaced from Colorado and my parents' lives began to undergo the slippages of middle age, I set out on my own quest for independence. Though my deepest and most indelible feelings remained imprisoned with my family, as behind a wall of thorns, I lived almost entirely away from home after the age of thirteen, when my parents decided, wisely, to send me to boarding school in Colorado Springs.

At twelve, and a scrawny twelve at that, I had got too far ahead of myself in the Boulder public schools. My classmates were fourteen or fifteen. While I could match wits with them in the classroom, they towered over me in the corridors and on the playground, the girls alarming in their new breasts and glossy hair, the boys strutting and swaggering with newly discovered pocket combs of sexuality. I became accustomed early to seeing nubile girls as members of an alien species, to be looked at furtively with fascination but not to be touched and hardly to be communicated with. My convictions of smallness, weakness, and frailty were enforced every day as, enviously, I watched the girls preening across the border of puberty. It did not lie in my power to bridge the gulf that lay between us. My only resource was to study harder, read more, *do* better. Thereby I merely emphasized my precocity, my differences, at an age when I wanted more than anything to be just like the others.

Teddie took special pains to encourage me to read on my own, weighing me down with recommendations of books to tackle, doling out from his library the novels of Stevenson, Kipling, Walter Scott, Charles Kingsley, and Dickens, which I read avidly. I could not share his enthusiasm for M. P. Shiel, Rider Haggard, G. A. Henty, and W. W. Jacobs. I chose my own bad books from the public library—Edgar Rice Burroughs and an interminable series of boys' stories about World War I entitled *The Boy Allies with the Cossacks, The Boy Allies at Jutland, The Boy Allies at Château-Thierry*. In these tales two young boys rode with the cavalry, sailed with the dreadnoughts, and advanced with fixed bayonets behind the tanks. It was reassuring to learn what these books taught: that the battle was not to the strong nor the race to the swift. Victory came to the boy allies because they were more mobile and inconspicuous than grown men. "Reeling back under the momentum of Captain Wigmore's charge, the hussars vainly strove to gather their stunned forces." Victory in the fray always fell to the more light-footed of the adversaries; the more stationary of the contenders always got the worst of it. Combat was settled by concussion, for all the world like jousting. The boys never received any harm worse than a flesh wound.

Playing with boys my own size bored me, for they were two years behind me in school; yet my schoolmates, except for a couple of social outcasts, showed no interest in playing football and baseball with someone my size. I was no longer of an age to play with my younger sister. One day, in a game of hide-and-seek, I found myself in the darkened gymnasium of the National Guard Armory down the street from my house with a girl my own age, a girl who the year before had been an expert tomboy street fighter. We hid behind the benches, but no one came to look for us. After a few minutes I wanted to get up and go, but something in the girl's manner told me that I must not. We lay there, not touching or speaking. Her breathing was strange, and I knew that something was expected of me, yet I could not make a move, for I hardly dared imagine what. We lay still for a long time under the Army banners hanging from the rafters, watching the cool dust sift slowly through the light from the high cramped windows.

I was strangled for the first time by the caught breath of desire, magnetized by its gravity, estranged by dread from this girl whom I had known for years and thought I understood as well as myself. Now she wanted me to touch and hold her freckled body, and I did not dare. Though the boys and I had groped one another as all boys do, testing the equipment, as it were, that had had little to do with desire, this sacred sexual terror. In all other matters my parting from my parents was gradual and delayed; in this, abrupt, total, and immediate. Nothing else in the conscious life of a child is vested with the awesome alloy of pleasure and fear that he finds when he first encounters the physical possibilities of love. I kept it to myself for a long time.

Going off to a boys' boarding school in Colorado Springs, which I did at thirteen, made this easier than it might have been otherwise. The Fountain Valley School was, then as now, situated at the edge of a shallow saucerlike depression in the plains about twelve miles southeast of the center of Colorado Springs. The pink stucco school buildings stood in an island of irrigated green in the huge dry land, which was dotted only by the cottonwoods that followed the course of streams and ditches. The country is still open today, but thirty years ago it was almost wild, unfenced, ranged by delicate antelope and scuttling prairie dogs, coyotes that yelped and howled at night when the moon was full, and rattlesnakes that basked in bare places under the sun. To the east spread limitless miles of tawny prairie; to the west the massif of Pikes Peak rose up fourteen thousand feet from the high edge of the plains, its snow rosy in the winter dawns and sunsets, its rock purple or brown in the changing light of the warmer seasons.

Amid this dazzling scenery a rich man's polo ranch had been taken over in 1930 for a boys' boarding school, Western in its attention to horses and mountains, Eastern in its Harvard-Haverford faculty and in its mores. In Boulder I had become used to facing both ways, and there was no change at the school: the Great Plains behind us led to the East, to our supplies of books and learning, but the irreducible mountains towered over us to the West. The school too was pulled in both ways: even the faculty suffered an instinctive division. The teachers of science and mathematics tended to look west to the mountains for their leisure time, for climbing, camping, skiing, and exploration; while the teachers of music, history, languages, and literature spent their summers in Massachusetts or Pennsylvania. The headmaster, Francis Froelicher, a taciturn and towering figure, climbed rock faces for sport but read us maxims from German philosophy and Quaker pacifism over breakfast. The boys rode horses in the afternoon and skied and climbed on weekends, but we dressed every night in blue serge suits, white shirts with detachable collars, and woolen school ties handwoven in Santa Fe, to dine in the flat-roofed Hacienda, with its thick adobe walls and floors of Spanish tile or polished wood, its patio garden and sumptuous furnishings. Overhead flew the warplanes from the nearby air bases of World War

II, while the school went in for farming to supplement the wartime food supply. On our rare expeditions into Colorado Springs to see *Return of the Mummy* or *Bride of Dracula* we found the streets swarming with uniformed men.

One of the principal advantages of Fountain Valley was its compactness. With only ninety boys I was able to get a sense of my place in the pack. Its high academic standards let me drop back a year, closer to my own age group. The Latin, mathematics, and English of my first year went easily, and I thus was able to turn much of my attention to team sports, to testing a physical mettle which I had had plenty of reason to distrust. I needed to feel I could make a team, could earn a place among my peers by my own efforts. It was less daunting to compete as one of a team of eleven than face to face, or in a fight. Making the team was the first challenge; helping it win was the second. How much less troubling it was to rejoice as one member of a group at having defeated a like-minded squad of uniformed and sweating young adversaries! Winning in this way was all right: it did not make me feel conspicuous. In one football game I had the chance to score the winning touchdown in a plunge through center, but I stumbled in the clear, alarmed by my sudden visibility, and fell without anyone's laying a hand on me.

My parents had made me aware from the beginning that my presence at boarding school was due entirely to the generous scholarship aid that Fountain Valley granted me. This was my privilege and my secret. (No one at the school, to its credit, ever mentioned the fact.) But I knew I had to surpass the other boys no matter how unpleasant I might find it to do so. Would winning not prove that I was well and strong, and therefore accountable? If I won at one contest, wouldn't a harder one be substituted next time? My letters home were full of this awareness, of mingled pride and anxiety as I bragged of what I had done and attempted to justify what I had not: "We had the first second-team basketball game of the season with the local Y on Saturday. The score was 24–23 with an overtime. Very thrilling, and I made the winning point. About twenty-five seconds to go, the score 23–23, and I am fouled and get a free shot. Amid thunderous cheers I stand and deliberately swish the ball through for a perfect basket, and we win, 24–23. It was very climactic."

The sexual imagery of this account was of course wholly unconscious, but this was perhaps the first victory that had ever belonged to my flesh, to me alone. Like my first success at masturbation a couple of months before, this triumph was truly *mine*. The calm strength of my arms, the "thrilling" and "climactic" sensations of my standing body, gave me my first hope, at fifteen, that the body could be a source of strength as well as a repository of weakness.

Masturbation, farting, belching, and other bodily functions were among our favorite boarding school preoccupations. At fourteen I had shared a room with a boy who, in a brave bid for fame, propped himself on his bed, kneeling, with his rump in the air, and achieved the school record, duly attested by witnesses, of one hundred and two consecutive farts. There were jousting matches in which, with one hand cupped and the other clawed, we attempted to grasp and twist one another's testicles. I could not help bragging of masturbation when I finally produced the longed-for effects. A few nights later, a group of giggling young monsters burst into my room after the lights were out and threw back my covers to expose me in my shame. The light blazed on and the cold air struck my heated nakedness at the same instant as their mocking laughter. I tried vainly to pull up the sheets as more and more faces appeared in the doorway. Such cruelties were routine, the concomitants of life in an all-boy community. The only sexuality we knew as yet was aggressive, and our humor was contrived to emasculate, to call attention to protrusions, noses, fat, hairiness, and the like.

When I contested impersonal standards or strove to please the older generation of teachers and coaches, I could imagine my parents in their place and did well because I was confident of pleasing. Direct competition with my intimates and equals, however, turned my knees to water. My fellows divined my self-distrust: though I had the poisoned gift of pleasing teachers, I was never elected to any office at school, no matter how minor. When I came within reach of my most coveted and hotly-trained-for prize, the victory in the school decathlon, the near prospect of actually taking first place and seeing my name emblazoned on the plaque as the 1945 winner suddenly made my strength drain away. Could I possibly deserve to win? I began, helplessly, losing. When it came to the last of the ten events, the quarter-mile, it became apparent I must take first place in my heat or run against the clock, if I was not to squander the whole effort. I sprang off fast and held a large lead for three hundred yards, but then I heard the pounding and panting of a competitor behind me, and I could think of nothing but the danger of being pursued, as in a dream. The footsteps gained, the hoarse breathing grew louder. My legs wrestled with my will and tried to make me stop and give up. Although I fell across the tape a step ahead of the other boy and thus collected just enough points to win the decathlon, I feared in my heart that my will to win had failed me, that the other boy, not I, had deserved the victory.

Most of my laurels fell in response to charm and a quick-witted answer, recognition of the sort that men give to bright boys. Yet I dreamed of talismans that would be freely granted me as a man by men, who would bow before my very presence like animals who know without sound or motion that they have met their master. Secretly, then, as when at sixteen I sat on the cliff ledge looking down into the abyss, I felt certain that triumph was only temporary, that ultimately failure would be my allotted portion.

2.

During the summer of 1944, just before my last year of boarding school, I got my first job, a summer appointment in the United States Senate as a page. My father had become acquainted, when they both received honorary doctorates from the University of Colorado, with the then governor, Edwin C. Johnson; my mother had beleaguered Johnson in her capacity as an officer of the Colorado League of Women Voters. Now he had moved on to the Senate for a while, and my father, in Washington, asked him if there was a summer opening for a page. Senator Johnson genially saw to it, and June 6, 1944, the day the Allied invasion of Normandy began, I sat in the Republican cloakroom of the Senate and watched Alexander Wiley (R., Wisc.) tap-dance in glee at the news. By the next day I had received my first Social Security card, signed an oath to protect the Constitution of the United States, and was rigged out in a page's uniform (black knickers with long black stockings, black shoes, white shirt, and black tie). I was assigned to the Republican side of the aisle, though Senator Johnson, like my parents, was a Democrat.

At nine-thirty each morning I reported for work and, once uniformed, helped lay out on the thirty-eight Republican desks the bills introduced, the previous day's *Congressional Record,* and other implements and documents. From noon until midafternoon, or even late into the evening during crises, we pages sat, each group on his own side of the aisle, on the steps at the foot of the rostrum, watching "our" side for a lifted senatorial eyebrow or a snap of the fingers or a peremptory gesture of need.

Our supervisor, an older boy, tended the telephones in the Republican cloakroom. There senators combed their hair, smoked cigars, and drank something called Poland water. They lay on sofas with their shoes off, napping, or walked about with yawns. We lingered in the cloakroom until driven out, for anything was better than sitting on the steps listening to the routine business of the Senate.

To avoid this we vied for the favor of the senior page, or "telephone boy," hoping to be sent on long errands to the House Chamber or the Senate Office Building (an errand known acronymically as an SOB), for such jobs might keep us away as long as an hour. When we could not escape, we learned to tune out the speaking voice of the senator who held the floor and focus instead on the true communications of the Chamber—the low buzz of senators murmuring to one another as they leaned together, the official reporters' pens scratching as they recorded the language that held the floor, the parliamentary conferences between the clerks, and the huddles among the powerful leaders and whips sitting at their front desks.

Outside the Senate Chamber on our errands we sauntered along the corridors of the Capitol paved with blue and red and ocher tile, as busy as village streets, past statuary commemorating heroism and statesmanship, threading through the herds of gawking tourists for whose benefit we would add a swagger to our walk. Doorways carried mysterious gilt legends: Sergeant-at-Arms; President of the Senate; Committee on Foreign Relations; Capitol Architect.

For the most part the pages lived an underground life, and

in those days a rather arduous one. They lived with their families or, occasionally, if their fathers were away at war, in boardinghouses. They had less time than most boys to indulge their adolescence, which may partly account for the precocious rise and fall of the notorious Bobby Baker, who was "telephone boy" in the Democratic cloakroom during my tenure. They regarded themselves as an elite and required stern rites of initiation for newcomers. Soon after I began work I was blindfolded, paddled with a broom, led up stairs and along mysterious echoing passageways, bound, and abandoned to the sound of giggles and receding footsteps. When I freed myself from my bonds I found myself inside the Capitol dome, above the vast rotunda where dead presidents lie in state. It took me the better part of an hour to find my way out.

The Senate, and the Capitol as a whole, reaffirmed the fact that Washington was a Southern city. All menial jobs were performed by Negroes, who worked in lavatories, in restaurants, as janitors. The pages were all white. The food in the Senate restaurant was uncompromisingly flavored for the palates of the Confederacy. The majority of Senate employees were Southerners, and the pace of their work, even at the height of the war in mid-1944, had a meridional and elderly leisure to it.

The Senate Chamber paid its devoirs to the past by keeping snuffboxes filled near the entrances. These were never used, except surreptitiously by the pages, who were given to sudden fits of sneezing on slow days. On each senatorial desk, beside the inkwell, stood a container of blotting sand. Within spitting distance of each desk was a shining brass cuspidor. Once, as I stood in the center aisle waiting for a senator to finish writing the note he wanted me to carry, I chanced to step between Ellison D. ("Cotton Ed") Smith (D., S.C.) and his hallowed spittoon. He narrowed his eyes, sensing my shadow, and let fly unerringly at my shoe.

If things got really slow, the youngest and most gullible page would be sent in search of a bill stretcher. His quest was met everywhere with the same bland, kindly evasion. "You say the Capitol Architect's Office sent you to me for a bill stretcher, sonny? Well, they ought to know over there that I've been out of them for a week or more. Why don't you try the House Archives? I think I saw some there lately. And if they're out of them, you might find a couple over in the janitor's office in the House Office Building."

Not much was to be learned about politics in the Senate during the summer of 1944. We stood in recess for some weeks while the presidential nominating conventions took place, the ones that selected Roosevelt for his fourth term and Dewey for his first try. Harry S. Truman was much involved with these affairs and did not spend much time in the Senate till the end of the summer, when his fellow senators crowded to congratulate him on his vice-presidential nomination, and he grinned back at them with his sharp teeth and his sharp nose and his sharp lapels and narrow shoes.

The Senate of 1944 had formed its temper during the administration of Woodrow Wilson, and by any standards its members were old men. The barons included Robert Taft and Arthur Vandenberg, Tom Connally and Alben Barkley. Most of the important legislation of the summer had to do with appropriations to be passed before the close of the fiscal year, or with farm price supports, or with price controls. If these matters were debated on the floor of the Senate at all, the language ran to the technical. The principal sound and fury, in crescendo as the elections approached, had to do with such questions as whether Franklin D. Roosevelt, as candidate for vice-president in 1920, had in fact wholeheartedly supported the League of Nations. Carl Hatch (D., N. Mex.) said yes, Styles Bridges (R., N.H.) said no. Was Hitler really wickeder than Stalin? Tom Connally (D., Tex.) said yes, Burton K. Wheeler (D., Mont.) said no. Should the Fair Employment Practices Commission be extended into peace-time? Theodore Bilbo (D., Miss.) said no, Robert Wagner (D., N.Y.) said yes.

Journalists have for years referred to the Senate as a "club," but without specifying that no club can survive without a staff of loyal employees who like working in the place. The Senate had a staff of hundreds, all appointed by personal influence, whose working life was given over to the task of making the senators comfortable, but the staff also formed a gallery for some senators to play to.

"A good senator," in the parlance of the help, was not necessarily a famous statesman or a power in the nation; he was a gentleman who deserved his place in the club, his seat on the aisle. Robert Taft and Harry Truman were "good senators," as was Carter Glass (D., Va.), who was ill and hardly put in an appearance all summer. Walter George, known as a leader in the country, was a "good senator," but so was Elmer Thomas (D., Okla.), whom few outside Oklahoma had heard of. Though Robert Wagner, author of the Labor Relations Act and other historic New Deal measures, was never referred to as a "good senator," Millard Tydings (D., Md.) was always included among the elect. "Goodness" referred to the senator's qualities of dignity, fairness, cheerfulness, manners, independence on matters that were not too controversial, willingness to compromise on matters that were; and, most important, seniority and a certain respect for the Senate as a body, and for the staff who worked below stairs.

While Eichmann loaded the cattle cars and MacArthur

landed on Leyte, I sat among the snuffboxes. It seemed a great distance from noon when, holding open the door of the Senate, I said, "Good morning, Mr. Vice-President," and Henry Agard Wallace replied, "Good morning, boys," to the more earnest realities of late evening when I plucked up my courage under the shadows of a magnolia to kiss Beverly Schafer good night.

Despite my lucking into the Senate job, I learned far less from it than I expected, only an easy skepticism about politics, certainly nothing that would help me in the confusing contest with myself. I found it comfortable enough to play the part of a boy running errands for older men, but it was a kind of service which might even become a specialty. I still wanted and needed to strive with my equals and come out ahead. All summer I dreamed of the plan to go mountain climbing just before school, a real adventure. It took only three days in early September to travel from the floor of the Senate to the high crags of the Crestone Needle, from the cigar-smoking faces of age and habit to the dizzying air of youth and purity. Yet as I climbed, at sixteen, I soon reached my known limits for the first time: those mountains rose as far upward and stretched as far towards the West, toward the New, as I would permit my life to take me.

3.

The thin air of the mountains, the vast gullied plains, had served my boyhood well, but in my last year of school I seethed with impatience to graduate into another country. I returned eagerly to my parents' cramped house in Washington and worried about whether I would be able to stand the gaff at Harvard. I spent the intervening summer, the last summer of the war, helping to supervise a playground near

Connecticut Avenue. I organized softball games, kept the wading pool chlorinated, taught the little children to swim. As an employee of the District of Columbia Recreation Department I was required to keep the black children of the neighborhood, who outnumbered the whites two to one, out of my playground and in theirs, a "separate but equal" facility around the corner, half the size of ours and lacking both shelter and supervision. Guiltily but stubbornly I refused to enforce infractions of the ordinance. On my last day I was given a direct order and shamefacedly obeyed it. Later that afternoon I heard the radio announce the news of the bomb that had struck the Japanese at Nagasaki.

It took me two years to learn what to make of Harvard. At first my reports home were even more conscientious than those I had written from Fountain Valley, full of resolve to Take Advantage of This Great Opportunity. I joined the Harvard Glee Club and was soon singing in concerts conducted by Koussevitzky and Bernstein and G. Wallace Woodworth. I studied my books with the ostentatious industry of those who are basically lazy and cannot work without the sense that someone is watching. I did not know what was required for success in this strange new world, and it never occurred to me to please myself, so I stuck to the formula of trying to satisfy my parents and my teachers. When I went home at Christmas I gave my father a hastily memorized little lecture on the philosophy of Spinoza, but it somehow only annoyed him.

Outside classes and activities I played either the bystander or the clown. I went to parties alone and joked with my friends' girl friends. A homosexual graduate student took an untoward interest in me, but I dodged it, not realizing that he found my behavior flirtatious when I had meant it only to be polite. My letters home were loud with vows and exclamations, some of them true, about the terrible pace of my academic work and the lack of time for rest. I quote one, more for its embarrassing period flavor than for the impression of earnestness it was trying to make:

You read and read and then write a little and find analogies and comparisons and consistencies and contradictions. And you find out what all the great men said about things and just where they were wrong and illogical and inconsistent and you see the bleak problems and fears so eloquently expressed by T. S. Eliot in his great poem *The Waste Land*. . . . And you hear the guys across the hall playing the radio and you wonder how they ever get any work done, and what they do with all their time, and you hear guys in the dining room telling with joy how drunk their roommates were last night, and you wonder why, and your friends plan a party and figure out who is going to take Bambi to the dance Saturday. And it's a beautiful day on the river and you give up and go outside and watch the crew row in their shells, and you waste two whole hours, when you should have read two books of the Bible so that when you're finished you can read the poems of Edwin Arlington Robinson and then get down to work on *The Republic* and you ask why you wasted all that time but you wanted to and it was such a beautiful day and you wish you could go into the country and just sit and look and smell sometime but you never have time because there's only two weeks left to reading period and you should go and see the Joneses but you have to work Saturday afternoon and there's a rehearsal every night this week and there is a play and a lecture and a concert all tonight which you want to go to and you have to pick your courses next year and they all conflict and there are eight you want to take but you can only take four and why don't those bastards next door turn down the radio.

Such studies were as pedestrian and slavish as my description of them. I ignored the excellent advice that my father had given me—to choose my courses for their teachers—and instead obeyed some greedy imperative to "cover the material" and "close the gaps." I did, in fact, just what Harvard told me to, absorbing not only what it offered me but its glib assumptions of the 1940s about the nature of education, its liberal-humanist outlook, its disinclination to distinguish between the vital and the trivial, along with its fair-mindedness and its honest attempts at "objectivity."

Only half aware of my reasons, in my second year I began to study the craft of verse. W. J. Bate, a magnificent teacher and scholarly devotee of English poetry, let me sit in on a graduate course in eighteenth-century neoclassic poetry, the most accomplished and tractable of our language and the most susceptible of close study by a mind frightened of its own depths. I was strangely excited by the lectures of I. A. Richards, being awakened by this greatest of teachers to the curious changes that language suffers under pressure, how words betray their users, how the life of language goes on independently of those who try to employ it for their own ends; how language dupes writers, and how it exalts them. Later on I read through the byways of twentieth-century literature under Howard Mumford Jones, in a copious and unorthodox course which taught a knowledge of bibliography and genre that would later prove indispensable to me as an editor.

When I arrived at Harvard in 1945, my classmates were all like myself, either too young for military service, or disabled. My friends at the outset were boarding school boys, mostly as it happened from Exeter. Later, after the veterans returned to the university from the war, Harvard became a very different and more exciting place. Many of the new entrants were years older than I and had traveled around the world. The friends of my first two years went on to become lawyers, architects, scientists, and businessmen. Thereafter I began to see more of an older group, most of whom were already trained as composers or aspiring to be writers. My new friends were publishing stories and poems in little magazines, were hearing their music performed at concerts in Cambridge, Boston, and New York, They did not need Harvard to legitimize their achievements, as I did.

I did not choose these new friends: they chose me. I was flattered and stimulated by the heady companionship of these older men. They invited me to share their rooms. We would often meet in Harvard Square in the mornings between classes and sit for an hour around a linoleum-covered café table drinking sweetish gray coffee and trying to come to grips with the evocations, the evasions, the issues that I. A. Richards had raised in his lectures on "the conduct of language," in which, seemingly concerned with semantics, he was really raising questions about the conduct of life. During these hours with Douglas Allanbrook, Dean Brelis, Seymour Lawrence, and others, I found myself struggling to use my mind for my own purposes; yet I couldn't yet understand what choices were available nor which of them my mind could be used for. Our formal education did not lead us in such directions. Magnificent teacher that Richards was, neither he nor my friends could have known how to advise a boy (even if he had asked for advice) who could not believe that his life was his own. I watched my friends' excitingly adult love affairs begin and end, but I could only observe, not participate. Mine was still a race, not a life, something to be won or lost, not lived. I was still accumulating characteristics by imitation and changing colors as fast as a chameleon so as not to have to decide which colors and characteristics were natural to me.

Through some of my friends I got to know many of the young composers, most of them trained by Nadia Boulanger,

who lived around Boston in the postwar years. Others introduced me to jazz at the Savoy with Red Allen and J. C.
Higginbotham. (The nightclub's doorman, I later realized,
was Malcolm X.) I joined the Signet Society, a quasi-honor-
ary undergraduate literary club, where I became acquainted
with those who would found the Brattle Theatre and the *Paris
Review* and go on to become actors, journalists, and writers.
The club included poets like Donald Hall and Robert Bly,
Kenneth Koch and John Ashbery (it occurs to me that none
of the Harvard poets of my time, including L. E. Sissman,
was a war veteran), whom I knew but shied away from as
though stung. Though I could bring myself to study poetry
as a subject, I associated the practice of the art only with my
father or older men like Robert Frost. I preferred not to
allow that poetry could actually be written by the young.

In the summers, when I went home to Washpa, I put
myself through further hoops of study but still managed to
avoid poetry by hook or crook. One summer I took a course
in philosophy at Washington and Jefferson, where my father
was dean, and also read through the syllabus of the English
novel from Defoe to E. M. Forster. Those summers, doubtless
because they afforded more leisure than my days at Harvard,
have left deeper scratches on my memory. I sat outdoors in
the late summer afternoons drinking beer while my father
beside me coughed and drank whiskey and talked about J. B.
Priestley and St. John's College, Cambridge, and J. C. Squire.
Here among the green Allegheny hills Teddie seemed more
nostalgic about England than ever. He had not been home
for almost twenty years, except for a few hours between
planes during the war. I built an unstable brick fireplace for
outdoor cooking and nursed the lawn while my father tended
his vegetable garden. My sister and I went swimming in the
hot lush afternoons. We spent much time together for we had

almost no friends who were not friends of my parents. There were no boys for my sister, no girls for me, except a pretty and lonely heiress of sixteen who lived in the largest house in town, at the top of the hill, and, had I only known it then, was dying to sleep with a Harvard man. My sister and I were sometimes bored by all the older company, so we made music together, and in the evenings I often practiced Schubert or Elizabethan songs with my mother after I had helped her with the dishes. But most of the time the house had visitors in it, members of the college faculty who dropped by for a drink and talked shop.

My life as a credit to the family was rich in emotion, but it was uneasy and confined to the four of us. At home we all made fun of ourselves, but in the world *out there* alternatives ranged only from the serious to the desperate. I fantasized over the myth of Orpheus, that psychic paradigm of the forms of contention between male and female. Through Gluck's version, Monteverdi's, Stravinsky's, Rilke's, Cocteau's, I brooded over the notion that both death and eternity lay at the heart of sex, that poetry could only be won by some fatal interchange, that the love of women must be bought by the death of the poet.

The relations between my parents horrified and fascinated me, but I thought instead of Orpheus and Eurydice or dreamed of encounters with eager princesses or pliant succubi, intermingling love and death with the ravening sexuality of adolescence. At Harvard I ransacked the fiction shelves of libraries and bookstores in search of scenes of seduction and surrender. Most of them remain more vivid to me still than the routine necking I sometimes performed on Saturday nights in hallways or darkened streets with half-willing girls. Nothing in real life could match the sleeping-bag scenes in *For Whom the Bell Tolls*, or ecstasies in the gamekeeper's cottage in *Lady Chatterley's Lover,* or the tawdry gropings and couplings of Dos Passos' *U.S.A.* In Ralph Bates' *The Olive Field* I read of a man urging a woman to surrender herself on a threshing floor or some equally titillating rural setting: "Give, woman, give, if you are going to do it!" Could I imagine myself ever saying anything like that to anyone? Let alone perform it?

I followed girls along the Harvard paths and Cambridge streets, devouring with my eyes the shapes of their bodies under the sway of their skirts, but if they noticed my admiration I had to look away or turn in to a shop. I tracked with particular fervor, one blazing autumn, a beautiful girl with shadowed eyes who always wore a yellow raincoat and tattered tennis shoes, and who seemed to be almost inseparably in love with a chinless person in tweed; yet I never dared speak to her even though I learned her name and chanted it to myself. How vividly I imagined their life together, the books and the record player in his room, the rumpled blankets of the bed, the skirt and blouse cast aside on a chair!

On a winter night, as I was following two girls along the brick sidewalks of Mount Auburn Street, one of them stopped and raised her skirt to hoist a stocking. Approachable! I thought. With my heart beating like a sudden drum, I marched across the street and asked, in a voice that did not sound like my own, "Can I help you ladies?" They looked amazed. "Help us? With what?" I had no second step planned. "Oh, nothing. I guess I made a mistake. Sorry." I turned away and tried to walk off casually, but their laughter echoed behind me in the dark street, and soon I was running.

When I was nineteen, I actually fell in love. She was a strikingly pretty girl from Radcliffe, who dressed in fawn and green and had straight brown hair in bangs that lowered her forehead and intensified her high cheekbones and the Aztec light of her eyes. I had known her for a couple of years, but she had recently taken on a turbulence, an unfocused intensity that excited me because I thought I was the source of it. The more ardently I pressed her, the more confusingly she drew away. We sat next to each other in classes. We kissed in the dark after dances. We wrote each other notes analyzing our feelings, our advances and withdrawals.

I insisted witlessly that our confused emotions sprang from frustration and that we ought to become lovers, that we would calm down in bed. She refused. Though she was easily excited, she was uncertain of the source of her excitement, and the harder I tried to seduce her (encouraged by the examples of my older friends' exploits), the more angrily we wrestled together, night after night. Finally what had begun in the liquid compulsions of ordinary desire turned into a dry, aching, ferocious combat that neither of us could win. I suppose it was a typical college affair of the period.

It reached its climax, though that is not exactly the right word, on a deserted beach in Duxbury on Memorial Day when we planned to picnic on the sand, but we never ate the sandwiches. Instead we grappled for hours behind a dune until our teeth were gritty, our loins ached with unspent tensions, and our backs were raw from frying in the unseasonable sun. I gave up in a fury, hating her for her refusal and myself for my incoherent persistence.

That summer she came to visit me in Pennsylvania. I might have guessed what would happen: she fell in love with my family instead of me, and for years afterward wrote them vague letters filled with yearning. It only went to prove once more what I had always believed: that authenticity existed only under my parents' roof. That disturbing summer of

1948, my twentieth, was the beginning of the end of my life at home. After my girl had left, one of my Harvard friends came to stay. He was older than I, and he puzzled me by managing to suggest that he thought of my parents as his equals.

Later in the summer we went on our last family vacation trip, driving our old car through Pennsylvania and New York State and New England, visiting various family friends along the way, to end up with a short stay in a rented cabin on Cape Cod. By the end of the summer it was clear we could no longer stand one another's full-time company. My sister quarreled horribly with my father, and we all took sides. While I spent the summer sheepishly tagging after my parents, my three college roommates were respectively studying in Europe, getting married, and serving (illegally) in Haganah during the Arab-Israeli war. I swore to myself, as I read D. H. Lawrence, that I must learn to live fully among my equals, to find love among my contemporaries and outside my family, to make my way with women. Independence was absolutely necessary, but to me, as to most of my generation, independence meant financial independence.

Just before returning to Harvard for my last year I spent a week at my grandmother's apartment in New York trying to come to a decision about what to do after graduation. I paid calls on friends of my parents and asked their advice. I talked to Wall Street lawyers, publishers, advertising men, journalists, and the representatives of foundations for foreign scholarships. An editor of *The Saturday Review of Literature* advised me to study economics. An advertising man told me that literary people were not the only interesting personages in the world, no matter what my mother said, but I could not believe he was serious. A book publisher told me that the primary qualifications for the trade were to wear your clothes well and be able to handle two or three martinis at lunch. A Columbia professor told me, disarmingly, by all means to go into book publishing because nobody with any talent was entering the field. I went to a downtown party in honor of Robert Penn Warren, where a graduate student in comparative literature told me that the American university student was doomed because of lack of artistic discipline, and I knew he meant *me*. I collected all kinds of conflicting and misleading advice about study abroad.

Despite all the advice I hadn't the faintest idea of what I *wanted* to do. I would graduate from Harvard before my twenty-first birthday. Perhaps I could travel abroad for a year and study something, or even (sinking feeling in the stomach) write? My grandmother thought she could finance a year abroad if I did not win a fellowship of some kind. So far, so good, but where would I go? Half thinking, I applied to my father's college, St. John's, Cambridge, and with that cheerful old-boy manner that used to be the Oxbridge habit, they instantly admitted me. I lackadaisically stopped applying to other places, taking the line of least resistance, which so often turns out to be easy to begin but painful to follow. When I finished Harvard I knew more than I knew, if less than I thought. As though my unconscious were telling me that the time had come for me to begin living, my handwriting had changed radically in the last two years and no longer looked like that of a child.

4.

After my father's death many years later, when I read the letters his friends had written him in his youth and the journals he had kept in vest pocket diaries in his delicate handwriting, I realized, somewhat tardily, that his three years at Cambridge had been the golden time in Teddie's life. He had left his mother in 1914 and lied his way into the Royal Navy when he was only sixteen, still six inches short of his full height. During his years of desk duty in London he read voraciously, and when the war ended he was singled out for government scholarship aid, even though he had dropped out of school at twelve. When he "came up" to Cambridge (for in English terms one "comes up" to the university and "goes down" to anywhere else in the world) he knew far better what he wanted of the place—to become a poet—than his younger contemporaries, products of a normal schooling and a conventional upbringing. For three years he had everything his way. He seemed to Cambridge in 1920, as I. A. Richards told me many years later, the likeliest candidate for the martyred Rupert Brooke's mantle as Young Cambridge Poet.

At the age of twenty-one my father had already published poems and reviews in *The London Mercury* and was writing much of what, half a century later, still looks like his best work. He took a First-Class Honours Degree in English Literature under Arthur Quiller-Couch, studied history under G. G. Coulton, edited *The Cambridge Review,* debated with such men as Denis Johnston in the Cambridge Union, acted under the direction of George Rylands in the Marlowe Society, entertained visiting celebrities like Vachel Lindsay, Walter de la Mare, Siegfried Sassoon, Hilaire Belloc, Sidney Webb, and Arnold Bennett. He had an intensely unhappy love affair and engagement. All the while he continued to write and publish poems, and his first volume, *Poems,* was published in 1920, when he was twenty-two. A year later he published a joint volume, *Four Cambridge*

Poets, with A. Y. Campbell, Frank Kendon, and the mysterious and gifted J. R. Ackerley, whose own posthumous autobiography, *My Father and Myself,* bore uncanny resemblances (except in its homosexual aspects) to the circumstances of my father's childhood. Though my father and Ackerley were friends, neither learned of the other's secret.

My father's Cambridge sponsor and patron was the poet and editor J. C. Squire, one of the first in a long series of older men my fatherless father worshiped. Squire was talented but lazy, a gifted parodist, a tireless versifier, for a time a brilliant editor and essayist. He founded *The London Mercury* in 1919 and published there the most noted older contributors in England: Yeats, Hardy, Conrad, de la Mare, and younger men like Edmund Blunden, Robert Nichols, Robert Graves; the Americans Vachel Lindsay and Robert Frost; essays by his European correspondent Mario Praz.

My father was one of the *Mercury*'s young discoveries, and Squire not only accepted and praised his poems, but sent for him and charmed him—as he was then able to charm almost everyone. Then, in a gesture that was as inexplicable as it was lavish, he offered to supplement my father's government grant out of his own pocket, to arrange for his admission to St. John's College, to pay his term bills and to supply an allowance. To my father, Squire was like an apparition from heaven. Long after Squire had lost his flair and had died, forty years later, an alcoholic, ruined, forgotten, my father was still not only reciting his name like a talisman (though no one remembered it) but defending Squire's memory against any real or imagined murmur of disparagement.

Any patronage as impulsive as Squire's was bound to have two edges. The promised money sometimes arrived at Cambridge, but often did not, a five-pound note here, a tenner there, but always a bit short of what my father had been counting on. There was something blandly sadistic in Squire's letters, scrawled en route in a taxi or between appointments at his office, couched always in a tone of external kindness and buried condescension. However, when Squire's friends and contributors visited Cambridge, he sent them to his protégé, and by the time my father went down at the age of twenty-four he was not only launched as a poet of promise, but widely acquainted as well with many of the literary luminaries of London.

Squire had set the example of tying the literary life to the leading-strings of social class. This encouraged my father to think of himself as "an English gentleman," to charge suits at tailors' establishments and run up bills with wine merchants, in short to adopt the life of the Edwardian "man of letters" at a moment in history when, as John Gross has written, the species was already moribund. But my father had no resources except talent, conscientiousness, and the considerable plausibility of his voice and his maturing presence. He served scrupulously as business manager of one London weekly paper and later as editor of another. He wrote reviews and poems, though the poems diminished in frequency and quality. His Cambridge friendships, especially those with J. B. Priestley, Frank Kendon, Gerald Bullitt, and Edward Shanks (Squire's assistant on the *Mercury*), grew deeper and stronger. Priestley, an indefatigable worker, was in these years writing reviews and essays for a variety of periodicals. Teddie shared a flat for a time with Priestley and his first wife. Soon after they moved out, Kendon and Bullitt moved in. The young men, ambitious for roles like those of Gosse and Saintsbury, Chesterton and Belloc and George Moore, talked endlessly of their work, their commissions, their métiers. But times were changing.

The vital center of written English was imperceptibly shifting from the London of Shaw and Wells to the Paris of Joyce and Gertrude Stein. Ezra Pound, moving to Paris after the war, showed the way, leaving T. S. Eliot behind in London as an increasingly influential outrider and archdeacon. The world of Squire and the world of Eliot were incompatible for social and cultural as well as historical reasons, and my father inevitably sided with Squire, while less worldly poets like Walter de la Mare and Edwin Muir never needed to take sides at all. Though in the 1920s there were many more book-reviewing media in London than now, the demand was falling. Priestley turned increasingly to novels and, later, after his gigantic successes with *The Good Companions* in 1929 and *Angel Pavement* in 1930, to the theatre. Bullitt wrote novels, not very successfully. Kendon, after several uncomfortable years, quietly gave up London to live in Cambridge and write fascinating and underrated poetry for the rest of his life. Shanks alone stayed on with *The London Mercury*.

My father was pure poet, ill equipped to turn novelist or playwright, and a better appreciator than a critic. Moreover, he was particularly vulnerable to the distractions of the literary-social life of London. His shadowy education, his social insecurity and his meager economic resources, his volatile temperament and his emotional cravings, all these combined to keep him engaged in a series of losing skirmishes against debt, and bound on a wheel of impulsive, quarrelsome, and inconclusive love affairs. In these he desperately demanded total fidelity in the same breath with which he hissed out his doubts and accusations. When he met, serenaded, and with his poor-boy's headlong yearning fell in love with my American mother, he was relieved to leave London behind and follow her to the New World.

5.

By the time I graduated from Harvard in 1949 and made
ready to sail for the old country, my father had been in
America twenty-four years. It had turned out to be easier to
sell himself—his presence on a platform, his efforts as an
administrator—than to practice his art. At fifty-one, in addition to poetry, he had had half a dozen creditable careers, as
professor, as lecturer, as reviewer, as director of the Writers'
Conference in the Rocky Mountains, in the military in
wartime, and now as dean of Washington and Jefferson
College. But in a complicated altercation of principle with
the trustees, my father, along with the president and a number of the faculty, resigned. In a single season he confronted
every anxiety that his past life had left him unprepared to
contend with. His foot slipped, and there were no more
fathers to give him a helping hand.

When I returned from Harvard, full of plans and expectations for a new life, I found my father frazzled and desperate,
full of bitterness after his three years of labor in an exhausting and uncongenial administrative job. Though the college
would give him a sizable terminal payment, he would soon be
out of work. He hadn't written a poem for years. His lecturing had gone stale for lack of practice. He felt that he had
bartered his promise, through a series of temptations as
subtle as they had been powerful, ever since his arrival in
America. My mother, after leaving her own career in Washington, had never been able to hide from him her distaste for
the internecine vendettas and the small-town gentilities of
college life in western Pennsylvania. At this moment he
looked up and saw me, his counterpart of thirty years before,
preparing to set out for golden Cambridge.

Drinking had always attracted my father when he was under pressure, and in the last months it had become a refuge. But whiskey could not wash away for long the bitter taste of himself. The night before I was scheduled to depart for New York and the S.S. *Washington* (how the name Washington reechoed through those years!), my mother gave her attention to helping me pack for the year abroad. Teddie, after a pint of Partners Choice Whiskey before dinner, found some pretext at the table to set off an unprecedented attack on his women. It made all quarrels of the last decade seem like child's play. His voice rose in crescendo to the unearthly screech of a wounded animal, as he denounced my sister for some awkwardness, my mother for indifference. As his rant intensified, he lurched back and forth in the semidarkness of the summer evening slamming doors and smashing crockery. He found my mother and sister, both thoroughly frightened, cowering together in a corner, and he began to rain blows on them.

Clearly words no longer meant anything to him. I felt every shriek in my stomach, but didn't know what to do. Six years before I had vowed never to become involved again, but now that it had come to blows I could no longer stay at my self-imposed distance. I made myself walk towards him through the shambles as he charged again to drive the women upstairs. I shouted, "Stop that, stop that, you can't!"

"Oh, can't I!" he shrieked, and stepped forward towards them once more.

Deliberately, with a sense of reaching down into the darkest regions of myself, I made my right hand rise from my side and, hard as it could, slap his face. My hand struck like a gunshot against the stubble on his flushed cheek. We stood glaring at one another, breathing hard, hearing still the sound of my mother and sister sobbing. He stared horribly at me, his eyes brimming with tears of shock and loathing and self-pity, and then he rushed from the house. I stood a minute longer alone with the enormity of my act, and then, my life suddenly recast, walked shakily into the hall to my mother and sister. I sent them upstairs and set about cleaning up the ruin of the house.

He did not return for hours, and when he did he was calmer, but stumbling drunk. I can no longer remember whether it was in the middle of that very night or the next that I set off in the family Oldsmobile to drive my mother and myself to New York, where she would see me off on the ship. She dozed in the seat beside me as though I was the unquestioned driver, and all night long we traveled along the Pennsylvania Turnpike and the deserted highways of York and Lancaster counties and New Jersey, to arrive in Manhattan at dawn in time for a few hours' sleep at my grandmother's apartment. The ship sailed at noon for Cóbh, Le Havre, and Southampton. I was nine days past my twenty-first birthday. My mother and I bade each other a sad goodbye. I would never return to Washpa: like Colorado and Washington, D.C., it would be trodden under. During my travels in Europe, my parents would move back to New York and live there for the rest of their lives. My future homes would be of my own choosing.

III

Back Out of All This Now Too Much for Us

Other poor fools in mirrors staring
Have tried to see behind the eyes
That watched them baffled and despairing.

One there was who, beyond all error,
Found what he looked for and grew wise—
Sufficient wise to smash his mirror;

And ever after walked avoiding
Windows and waterpools wherein
His secret might have leapt from hiding.

But I, ignorant still, and cheated,
Gaze on my glassed and cryptic twin,
And he looks back at me defeated.

Edward Davison, "The Secret"

Mirror, mirror on the wall,
Who is falsest of us all?

Only silence. Does this mask
Hear no questions mirrors ask?

P. D., "Sacrificial Mask"

1.

When I disembarked at Southampton I was hailed at the pier by my father's oldest friend from the early days of World War I. He was a lean, tweedy, pipe-puffing manufacturer of luxuriously fitted picnic hampers of the sort the royal family might use for Ascot or grouse shooting. He and his daughter piled my luggage and me into his car and drove, via Winchester, to his fourteenth-century thatched cottage in the Sussex South Downs. I spent a week there, in the most English of all possible surroundings, regaled with tea before breakfast, beer before lunch, tea before sunset, and gin before dinner. We went for walks down the lanes and over the Downs, through the beech forests of Arundel and the back alleys of Brighton. We visited many of my host's friends. As I listened to them talk I began to discover in my mouth, like fishbones, the implications of the British class system. It began to dawn on me that these Englishmen identified one another through voices and intonations, not through manners or actions or opinions. Americans in Colorado had always thought my father's accent "snooty," and in a sense they were, of course, right. His intonations identified him socially and he knew it.

I could hardly believe what I began to discover about the English. I encountered outspoken anti-Semitism face to face, and my half-Jewish innocence felt it like a blow. My pulses within a week were already hammering with fury at the costive middle-class frigidity that I had only read about in E. M. Forster and D. H. Lawrence. I bit my tongue while my hosts gave me little lectures on the importance of race and the unmistakability of breeding. Nobody had warned me about this.

My next stop was London, where I was met by my shy, intelligent, diminutive uncle at King's Cross Station and driven to the northern suburbs to stay with him and his wife, my father's strapping and uninhibited younger sister. The atmosphere could not have been more different from Sussex. Aunt Amy whistled and clattered about the kitchen of the semidetached suburban villa with its little rectangle of garden in back. While she scorched the pots and desiccated the food in time-honored English style, she chattered on and on to me about her adored, misguided, glamorous, quarrelsome older brother. She introduced me to Teddie in his youth. I found him difficult to recognize—foolish in love, overgenerous in friendship, vulnerable to disappointment, and her secret sharer in the pain of their childhood. She went on to unfold, tactless and unfettered, her view of the whole generation that had surrounded my father before he left England. Within a few days of my arrival at her house she exhumed twenty-five years of my father's early family history and his private life, everything that for whatever reason he had chosen to keep dark. Under the circumstances I found it heady stuff. Amy understood Teddie as perhaps only a younger sister could. She had known him without any of the trappings of family and fatherhood, without the mantles of professorship or the regalia of military life, without any of the rewards and punishments that America had given him.

She had, however, not laid eyes on him for many years and was never to see him in his adopted habitat.

I also met my English grandmother, a frail but tough little creature, now about eighty, who lived in one room of an apartment not far from Aunt Amy's house. When I first went to call, she had put on her hat for the occasion, a black straw circlet adorned with paper flowers. She sat erect in her chair without touching its back with hers, and she was at first very stiff with me, shy perhaps, perhaps alert to signs of disapproval. But after an interval she began to discourse on the topics of the day, complaining about the crime everywhere, the prevalence of strikes, the helplessness of government under the socialists. "When I was a girl," she said proudly, "the Prime Minister would have called out the lancers. If Mr. Churchill were still in power, he'd do it. That would show the people!"

By the side of her chair, on the bureau, stood a photograph of a man with a shiny face, a large round nose, and a moustache, dressed in some sort of ceremonial garb, an alderman's costume, as I later discovered. This was my late grandfather Shields, and I asked about him. "Oh, he was such a wonderful man. Everybody loved him. And he had such a beautiful voice, he sang so sweetly. He was such a good husband to me. I miss him every day of my life, and I pray for his soul every night and morning."

She insisted, on this first meeting, that we go for a walk in the neighborhood, and she steered me directly to the local Anglican church, where she introduced me to the vicar. As we left, she said, "Now when are you going to be baptized?" She was clearly worried that my parents had neglected my religious instruction. Each time we met that year she dwelt on this subject, and, although I avoided any direct answer, the repeated inquiry had an effect on me, a sort of disturbance within.

Once I took her to an elaborate meal at Simpson's-in-the-Strand, where she sat in her shabby coat with regal indifference as waiters deferentially helped her to slices of roast beef from the silver-lidded serving tables. It was her first trip into the heart of London in many years. While we ate she spoke of what a magnificent man Teddie was, and what a good son he had been to her. Despite the hardships of her life, her innocence was still bright.

My next visit was to the Isle of Wight and the house of J. B. Priestley. A baronial establishment, it looked out over the sea and along chalk cliffs from the top of a steep slope of gorse and bracken which swept half a mile down to the water —too much of a view for comfort perhaps. The house lay in Tennyson country, a place of cliffs and lighthouses, of ruins and ancient rings of trees, planted for prehistoric rituals, strange swales and lanes and heights and views and winds. Hopkins' "The Loss of the Eurydice" kept coming into my head: "Now Carisbrook keep goes under in gloom;/ Now it overvaults Appledurcombe."

The great stone house, of Edwardian vintage, was handsomely and comfortably got up with good furniture, paintings by Utrillo, Augustus John, and the English watercolorists, a billiard table and a player piano on which my feet ground out, *con moto,* Schumann's "Carnival." The house was teeming with family, friends, servants. Both Priestley and his then wife Jane had been married before, and their six children came in force, bringing their families and friends for visits.

I could not get used to the English country house atmosphere and rituals. Breakfast was sumptuous, brisk, with hot dishes of kidneys or kippers on the sideboard at a stated hour.

Priestley disappeared and wrote all of every morning at the very least. His wife also disappeared to go over the accounts of their vast farm, supervising not only the housekeeping but the tenants, overseers, and bailiffs, the Galway and Guernsey cattle. The children disappeared into the surrounding countryside to visit friends, or simply to undiscoverable regions upstairs. I went to my room and desultory readings in Goethe's *Faust*. In the afternoons there would be fierce tennis on the private court, tea on the terrace, cocktails, and late lavish dinners. After meals everyone vanished again. I didn't quite know what to do with myself or what to say, for whatever popped out seemed to bristle with gaucherie. When left alone I fidgeted up and down the empty halls and outdoors along the lanes and garden paths, not knowing whether to hope to encounter some gardener to talk to, or whether to hide behind a tree till he passed.

2.

Within two days after leaving the Isle of Wight I launched out on my first real journey: being a credit to the family was not the issue this time. I took a train for Italy, through northern France and Basel into Domodossola and through the Po valley to Bologna, Florence, and Siena. There I stepped out of the English language, living in a musicians' *pensione* and speaking a babel of Italian, French, and German. The other inmates were all students at the Accademia Musicale Chigiana. My college roommate, Douglas Allanbrook, was studying the harpsichord with Ruggero Gerlin in master classes. I was allowed to sit in for two or three hours each morning while the students were prompted in Bach preludes and fugues and Scarlatti sonatas.

I wandered on foot through labyrinthine medieval streets,

past doorways of beaded curtains, through the southern smells of freshly ground coffee, *vespasiani,* fruit and wine, in and out of cool striped churches. I gazed from the town walls over the glaring Tuscan landscape with its fields of pale yellow corn, its terraces of silver olive and black cypress, its dusty roadsides and rutted tracks rigidified by the August heat. I went to concerts and rehearsals, in rooms loud with clavicembali and wooden flutes, vocalizations and glissandi. I slept in a high dark chamber with imitation Pompeian ceilings and chilled marble floors. I squatted every morning in a ripely malodorous *gabinetto* and wiped myself with newspaper. I drank cool white wine till my eyes glazed and my head buzzed. My tongue slithered through festoons of pasta and the pink flesh of figs and the balm of strong warm oil.

On travels here and there in Italy I met an unembittered former German prisoner of war in a train; a half-reformed prostitute who looked like the goddess Diana, helping to keep house in my Siena *pensione;* a wild-haired violinist spouting Roman dialect (he would in later years turn into a very tame conductor); a young American ballerina named Tanaquil Le Clercq traveling alone and inclined to romance; a bearded French mime with a lovely girl who moved into our *pensione* and baffled me by his matter-of-fact Frenchness. I visited George Santayana, who sat in his cell in the Convent of the Blue Nuns in Rome with nothing around him except a few books and a reproduction of Fra Angelico, and talked about little except money; I accompanied Nadia Boulanger as she took the steps to the top of the unfinished Siena Cathedral two at a time and exclaimed at the marvels of the view; I met a young peer of the realm who borrowed money on Capri and faithfully paid it back later in London. (Years afterwards I discovered he had lent Dylan Thomas hundreds of pounds and never saw a penny again.)

All these impressions, added to the wonders of the Piccolomini Library or the Siena Pinacoteca or the Duccio "Maestà," the chill stone streets of Siena and the skull-cracking August sun, revived my eyes and ears and aroused my unwashed skin. I recovered sensations I had forgotten since the years when I had clambered over desiccated grass and sliding shale in search of the ultimate purity of mountain water, built my first nesting place among the high spruces, and leaned down to drink from the brook with cupped hands. If I was fleeing from my father and his England, I had little doubt of what I was looking for. Two weeks to the day after leaving London I at last found myself in bed with a woman.

For some people, of whom I was one, the first serious sexual experience sets up disturbing reverberations. Here was something mysterious and overwhelming that could not be worked at, could not be guided. It simply emerged from what I was and what I had been. I *was* what I *wanted*. There was no difference between me and it. Yet the exaltation of the senses, of fingertips and moisture and smoothness, could not silence anxiety. The girl was an old friend, the former lover of another friend. She was beautiful, willful, insecure, and she bore a sometimes uncanny resemblance to my mother. We were physically ill suited, and my awakening, despite her generosity, was far from complete. Nevertheless, the intensity of my own sensations frightened me with their newness. Could the body survive such turbulence? Far from quieting me, physical love opened terrifying and unsuspected energies.

As she and I lay in bed or wandered through the alleys and passageways of Venice, I immortalized my parents' quarrels by restaging them (with the girl's assent and even connivance). It was a strange and disarming coincidence that we should both regard sex as a bone of contention, and should both accept music as a healer, as though the cells of our minds had been stamped with the scars of the generation who had fought in the sex wars before we were born. When I took her to the Venice railway station at the end of our few days together, we parted as two friends who had shared a journey and an encampment but not yet ourselves. It was not surprising, perhaps, that I should be confused by the paradoxes of this experience; yet my principal anxiety at the time was not the nature of my feelings, but their violence. Could so painful a tempest of emotion conceivably be the only alternative to the gnawing ache of loneliness? Was I condemned to repeat everything in my parents' lives—the quarrels too?

I found I still believed that only *their* feelings could be regarded as authentic, that mine could merely follow palely on their heels. Now I had reason to fear that sex too, like anger and guilt, pride and ambition, the eloquence of poetry and music, above all like the capacity to inflict pain, could never be exercised as my own possession without my parents' endorsement. How could it be otherwise when the only record of my experiences was being submitted for my parents' daily approval?

Before I left home I had promised to keep in touch. Rather than letters I would write an informal journal of my travels and send it home at least once a week for safekeeping. It seemed like an innocent enough pursuit, but the journal-keeping turned into an exercise of a very different color, almost sinister. I poured all my experience and capacity for observation into telling my parents everything I did, though not quite all I thought. It was the last form of writing exercise I needed. After my parting quarrel with my father any gift I sent home was bound to be poisoned.

In actual practice, the journal was thumbed and scrutinized and read aloud around the family breakfast table in New York, and my parents wrote me their bright, concerned comments on it. Far from fulfilling its intended purpose as a written declaration of independence, the hundreds of pages added up to a second mortgage. Just as the wandering student rebel quietly accepts checks from home to support his revolution, so I needed nourishment from the one source to which I dared not reveal my appetite. I did not yet know that I could never become a writer so long as I thought of my parents as the "audience" for my writings. Nor, until I could recognize my own emotions as genuine, would I be able to qualify as a lover. My parents' shadow lay between me and the sun, yet I could muster neither the strength nor the need to get free. Each of us is aware in some corner of his consciousness when the time has come to rise over the next hurdle of his life. I saw the hurdle approaching as I ran toward it, I strained every muscle, I balked. I could not make myself jump.

Throughout the year of my "freedom" I wrote hundreds of words in which I bragged like a child of my accomplishments, swaggered in the newness of my experience, recounted the details of a couple of dreary encounters with prostitutes, anatomized the groggy tactics of a useless Cambridge flirtation, listed books read and concerts attended, museums visited, people met—and bound myself closer to home by every word. Even my confessions were tossed off with an air of tinny bravado, as though I were demonstrating that the collector of diplomas and scholarships was also capable of collecting *fleurs du mal* as part of his official education. Would nothing I wrote ever persuade my parents that I was dangerous? Alas, no. They found my journals so *interesting*.

3.

At Cambridge I was assigned "modern" rooms (that meant
they had central heating which did not work) in my father's
college, of course: the master had been his tutor. St. John's is
a rambling complex of Gothic, Tudor, neoclassic, Neo-
Gothic, and county-council-modern architecture, one of the
biggest colleges at Cambridge, famous then for its rowing.
The dons were of variable distinction, but I was lucky
enough to encounter a group of English undergraduates who
were my equals both in age and in learning. I saw few
Americans.

Cambridge in 1949 still retained most of what must be
counted one of the glorious luxuries of education—a consum-
mately beautiful, relatively remote, and reasonably inexpen-
sive system of residences in which specially selected young
men could circulate as energetically or idly as they chose, and
educate one another. The system had its dangers—intellectual
dilettantism and social arrogance—but more than any other
institution I have known, Cambridge relied on the utopian
principle of Rabelais's Solesme, *fay que vouldra*. James D.
Watson's *The Double Helix* evokes Cambridge's special as-
sumption that almost anything could be managed without
betraying evidence of excessive effort.

Before coming to England I had planned a "research
project," a study of the climate of Georgian poetry before
and after World War I, my father's period. I worked on it a
little, but I never completed it. Sometimes I went to lectures.
I read voraciously in modern literature—fiction, poetry, psychoanalysis. I went to the theatre often, both in Cambridge
and in London, and to the Royal Ballet. I made music. But
mostly I talked with friends, especially Peter Shaffer and

James Mossman. Their conversation was woven out of whimsy, out of disemboweled clichés. They improvised skits built on the anomalies of English class discrimination, the absurdities of academic life, the pomposities and hypocrisies of the old. The style was not unlike that of Stephen Dedalus and Buck Mulligan in the early part of *Ulysses.*

Peter Shaffer had come up to Cambridge after several years working underground in the coal mines, where both he and his twin brother, Tony, had been drafted as "Bevin boys" in an alternative form of national service. As a result he was improbably muscular, though gaunt of face and nervous in action. His conversation had a way of beginning with some mumbled absurdity, as his eyes shifted uneasily behind his glasses. He was edgy until assured of an amused hearer. Then, with the least encouragement of a smile or laugh, he was off and running, his wit unleashed, babbling, snickering, mimicking. While he could on occasion talk with deadly, even sentimental seriousness, much of his normal talk ran to a wickerwork of mockery, Restoration epithets, and throw-away imprecations. He was musical, febrile, emotionally open and terribly vulnerable, gnawing himself to pieces with recurrent peptic ulcers, a theatrical word-dazzled man. He was not yet the masterly playwright he would become, but a parodist, a translator, a would-be novelist perhaps, though helplessly stage-struck. Peter and I went to a series of lectures together, but our attendance degenerated into a lot of silly note-passing, and as I lost interest in formal study, I gave lectures up. But we saw each other often.

Peter, Tony, and their younger brother, Brian, had begun to concoct their world of fantasy and parody long since, in the nursery. At Cambridge it became extended and elaborated. With a large cast of characters, a full orchestration of male and female voices, a collapsible set of slapstick jokes, they kept up an incessant tattoo of nonsense. It was the safest attack on their parents' world, the humbug of things as they were.

One game that embodied all these impulses went under the name of "Snivel," fantasy after fantasy ridiculing the dreariness of British postwar life. A snivel was an Englishman, usually lower-middle-class, obsequious with his betters, not young, given to a diet of cold pork pie, turnips, cabbage, and terrible pink teacakes. Snivels were the drab patient people who would wait all day in a queue to catch a bus to Clapham or Chalk Farm. Snivels never complained about their lot, feeling that it was all for the best. They sat around tiny blue gas fires on cold nights as they ate their revolting food. Their work was as glum as their play. They doted on the royal family and devoured newspaper serial excerpts from the memoirs of "Crawfie," governess to the princesses Elizabeth and Margaret Rose.

It was the long-suffering staunchness of sniveldom, of course, that had brought England through the war and enabled it to endure the drab peace that followed, but the Shaffers could not abide the postures it had created, the very attitudes of patience and resignation that would infuriate Jimmy Porter a few years later in *Look Back in Anger*. During the winter of 1949–50 rationing was still in force for meat, eggs, sugar, butter, fuel, and gasoline. There was nothing for it but to keep on suffering slightly, even after ten years of worse.

The fashionable life style of Cambridge then was what came to be known later as *camp*. Those bright young men who were not in fact queer pretended to be. There was no way, besides actual experiment or asking very rude questions, of telling the knaves from the queens. I was fairly sure that they couldn't *all* be gay, but not quite sure. Homosexuality had no appeal for me, but I was all too aware that one of the reasons I seemed to have little trouble getting along in this society was that some members of it were drawn to me. There were of course girls at Cambridge, at Newnham and Girton, but they were badly outnumbered and far from appealing. Given my own uneasiness, physical sex, it seemed, would just have to be put off for a while longer. What I did not have, I thought I would not miss, and my friends seemed to be as celibate as I. Instead of sex, we played our complicated verbal games—Snivel and its counterpart, the Mossman Game, which looked more serious on the surface but had, perhaps, less real point.

Jim Mossman, a long-time friend of Peter Shaffer's from St. Paul's School days, was as closed emotionally as Peter was open, though he was equally lighthearted. Mossman was extremely tall, handsome in a lantern-jawed way, self-possessed, blandly courteous. Each time I met him he seemed just to have witnessed some extraordinary scene on the street—a little gnarled man who had been riding a bicycle backwards in order to disprove the Theory of Relativity; a limp-wristed aesthete of unbelievable affectation, drawling to a friend, "But—my dear—since discovering *women* I never use anything *else*"; two corpulent dons in full academic dress arguing like sumo wrestlers over the Arian heresy in the High Street. He was a hilarious mimic and storyteller, but also—an unusual combination—an eager questioner and listener.

Jim's father had been killed in World War II. Not long afterwards Jim had left St. Paul's rather than inform on a fellow student, an act of integrity which had made him famous. At Cambridge he worked, when he worked, with a fine analytical distrust of the conventions of historical scholarship, but he kept finding the same burglar under every bed: "The curse of Western history is self-consciousness." Despite months of discussion, I never learned just what was meant by this notion, but it was lodged in Jim's mind like a bullet. In endless arguments, we traced the development of Western languages, literature, and social institutions to see how many of the world's present discontents could be laid to "the degeneration of instinctual responses." Science, technology, and ultimately psychoanalysis, Jim argued, had illuminated the recesses of man's mind, forcing the individual to become more "aware" of himself and diminishing the "natural" relationship between man and society. Every conscious effort to make man conform (socialization, enlightenment, material progress) was doomed to make matters still worse by raising expectations and creating deeper discontent.

Jim believed this literally, not simply as a yardstick for historical study but as the explanation of individual behavior, his own and others'. As the year wore on and he forced every conversation back to the same gnawed bone, I became increasingly perplexed, for it was my first encounter with the excessive piety of the convert, the monomania of the dispossessed. How could so intelligent a man be guided by a worldview of surpassing banality and hold to it with the fatuous tenacity of a hypnotized hen? I was baffled, but then I was only just discovering the English. Jim had not only the cardinal virtue of the cultivated Englishman (the capacity to reconcile opposites by ignoring them) but also the cardinal fault—an inability to meet logic at the last ditch. I discovered him to be desperate for love but too withdrawn to admit it to very close quarters. He was frank in his homosexuality, especially in later years. He seemed unable to respond physically to his intellectual equals, preferring to cruise in pursuit of young trade with sloping shoulders.

I kept in touch with Jim in the years afterwards. He went for a while to the Foreign Office, then turned journalist and television interviewer, and finally novelist as well. After I became a publisher, my firm brought out the American editions of his novels. He retained his views on self-consciousness and history till the end of his life. It came in May 1971, a week before the publication of his novel *Lifelines,* by an overdose of sleeping pills. Jim had been alone in his Norfolk cottage, and left a note for his brother which the newspapers quoted: "I cannot stand it any more, but I don't know what it is." Perhaps it was the internal contradictions of an English life. His personal conduct had been polarized between the amused stoicism of a traditional English gentleman and the self-deprecating camp of a screaming queen. The two could not be reconciled forever. Jim was condemned by the English entanglement with language, by the way her institutions identified him instantly, the moment he opened his mouth, as a member of the upper middle class, though his humanity, his inner life, took place underground. His plight was not so very different from George Orwell's—or from my father's.

4.

At Cambridge I began at last to clamber onto the first of the plateaus that education can grant: where a certain confidence in the power of one's mind to comprehend simple intellectual problems is mingled with a reasonable respect for what is mysterious and unreachable by mere knowledge. But I was walking along the boundaries between my father's generation and my own. Only now did I begin to sense that my "choice" of Cambridge might be as suspect, as equivocal, as my father's nostalgia. The terrible scene the night before I left America kept rising before me. The fact that my blow had been necessary did not lessen my guilt. I had become aware that part of me hated my father, and I now faced the grim knowledge that my hatred was nothing new. It became harder, as I learned more of the truth about England, to conceal my feelings. Each installment of my Cambridge journals included some thinly veiled aggressive gesture, a smaller slap, a dose of caustic corrective. After meeting my father's friends, I recorded how old they were looking. After lunching at pubs he used to haunt, I noted how run-down they had become. When I encountered his surviving Cambridge heroes, I described how stuffy the undergraduates found them now. Then I mailed the pages home.

I went uneasily to see the Man of Letters, Sir John Squire. He was living in a tiny two-room flat near Victoria Station in London. He greeted me at the door wearing white flannels. Whether he had just come from, or was just going to, a cricket match I don't remember, but cricketer's pads and gloves and bats lay heaped in a corner. By this time he must have been in his sixties, bald on top with a generous fringe of gray around the ears. Nose red. Eyes close-set. He waxed expansive and offered me a sherry as though we were seated on a divan in the Reform Club instead of on a day bed in a dump. We spoke of my father and of Cambridge. A buxom young woman walked in without knocking. Squire introduced her as his secretary.

When I rose to go, he asked me to come and see him again, but I never found him in and he never answered my letters. Not directly, at least. Twenty years later I found that Squire had written my father immediately to describe my visit. The letter spoke of me with great enthusiasm, with a glow that had never warmed the slightly patronizing communications of a generation earlier, written from the editor's desk and enclosing money. This letter of Squire's, generous as it was, may have graveled my father as he sat in furnished rooms in New York, mourning his past and waiting for someone to offer him a job. But it also gratified him, I am sure, for he was never jealous of my successes (of which he would surely have counted Squire's approval one), and we always pretended that neither he nor I had ever known failure.

So it went during that autumn. After the sensuous summer of Italy, the cold damp winter of England. After a couple of months of foot-loose traveling, a return to the student's lockup. After what seemed the ultimate break away from my family, a gradual realization that my journals bound me to them more powerfully than ever, that whatever I wrote was written for them to read. After my first love affair, a regression to celibacy in a society where the most intense sexual activity seemed to be homosexual. Where was my freedom?

About six weeks after arriving at Cambridge I hit the hurdle I could not jump. My signal was notification that I had been granted one of the first Fulbright scholarships, enough to cover the cost of my Cambridge studies. After a flush of pleasure I was shocked: once again I was being rewarded for the wrong reasons, for being a slavish imitator rather than an original, a boy not a man. I was sick of education, yet money came to me for extending it. What I really wanted to do was write something of my own, but all I could bring myself to do was to compose disguised letters to my parents. I was absolutely disgusted with the taste of myself.

I was seized with the impulse to flee everything I had gained, to relinquish everything academic, everything inherited, everything English, to go somewhere else, anywhere, without encumbrances, to live on an island like Robinson Crusoe and "be myself." I was in the destructive mood, when the urge comes to smash everything one has received from other hands.

I felt I had no one to turn to except all these men who talked and talked, who played games that meant nothing to me. I had no one I could trust to love me. My oedipal reflex in repudiating my father was to embrace the love of women, but there were no women available. The child in me was enslaved. Even my new-found money could be mine only if I stayed on at Cambridge and carried on with my study of the poets of my father's generation. I felt more tightly bound to the wheel than ever, as though I could not help fulfilling Teddie's expectations and repeating his failures. I could not sleep, I could not study, I could not write. In my panic all I could think of was to throw it all away, to get out. The fact that Teddie wanted me to write made it all worse, for I could not defy him without denying myself. At Cambridge, three thousand miles away from home, I felt my family's hot breath. To become able to write I would have to mount a successful rebellion against my father; but since there was nothing he wanted me to do more, rebellion presented a logical impossibility.

So I entered my "identity crisis." The phrase was not yet current, nor had the event itself become so predictable as to be budgeted for. Rebellion had not yet become a social convention. I had, however, come across one experience in literature that had certain similarities with my own, and I remembered John Stuart Mill's description in his *Autobiography:*

It was in the autumn of 1826. I was in a dull state of nerves, such as everyone is occasionally liable to; unsusceptible to enjoyment or pleasurable excitement; one of those moods when what is pleasure at other times becomes insipid or indifferent; the state, I should think, in which converts to Methodism usually are, when smitten by their first "conviction of sin." In this frame of mind it occurred to me to put the question directly to myself:

"Suppose that all your objects in life were realized; that all the changes in institutions and opinions which you are looking forward to, could be completely effected at this very instant: would this be a great joy and happiness to you?" And an irrepressible self-consciousness distinctly answered, "No!" At this my heart sank within me: the whole foundation on which my life was constructed fell down. All my happiness was to have been found in the continual pursuit of this end. The end had ceased to charm, and how could there ever again be any interest in the means? I seemed to have nothing left to live for.

I did not, however, remember the event that enabled Mill to snap out of his depression.

. . . A small ray of light broke in upon my gloom. I was reading, accidentally, Marmontel's *Memoires,* and came to the passage which relates his father's death. . . . A vivid conception of the scene and its feelings came over me, and I was moved to tears. From this moment my burden grew lighter. The oppression of the thought that all feeling was dead within me was gone.

Even if I had remembered the second passage, I doubt if I was capable of realizing what was troubling me. The violence I had done my father had somehow become tangled with the violence of my feelings during my Venice love affair. Sex and rivalry were two strands in the same rope, a rope that seemed to be strangling me. There was nothing to do but wait for the crisis to pass, or to flee before it.

Perhaps I would have been better off eventually if I *had* run away, if I had made a place for myself somewhere without any help or interference from the past. This might have forestalled some other evasions in the future. But as it happened I found someone whom I could talk to about my problem and who persuaded me to stay. It was Peter Shaffer, whose relations with his family, though profoundly different from mine, hung upon him as painfully as mine did. I found he too had been through his times of agony and that even if he could not yet deal with his own adult problems he was capable of being a compassionate and sympathetic friend. He listened to my incoherent miseries and undertook to distract me by taking me for walks, telling me stories, going to the movies with me, and diverting my attention from myself once I had eased my burden. No one could have been more devoted or attentive. I suspect that Peter's effectiveness in this situation may have surprised even him. As the weeks went by and my crisis began to pass, I felt exhausted and dissipated, but at least I had found a friend whom, even though he was much more talented than I, I could love as an equal and need not distrust as a rival.

At Christmas I visited the Priestleys again. Of course I had written my parents about my troubles, and my father had suggested I ask Priestley's advice about whether to leave Cambridge. Priestley urged me to stay, to take the Fulbright money while I had it but to ignore all requirements and do as I pleased for the rest of the year. It was good advice, especially since I could take it as coming from a father surrogate. Although the winter saw me no happier than I had been, the crisis gradually receded. A dream which came to me later on shocked me but at least primed my consciousness.

One night in my sleep I found myself on a streetcar in Washington, D.C. (that prettiest and most frigid of cities), bound to visit the girl with whom I had slept in Venice. After getting off the trolley car, I made myself walk away from the tracks up a hill to my left. The way grew steeper. I neared the top of the street, searching eagerly for the house I wanted, and came face to face with my mother. She looked at me pityingly, as though she knew something I did not. When I asked her the trouble, she hesitatingly told me, as though against her will, that I was impotent. I could not believe her, but she repeated it again and again, crooning and chanting about the beauty of women's bodies "down there," almost exulting that I would never be able to know the fulfillments of sex. I awoke, shuddering from the fears I did not know I had been containing all this time, the classic fears of rivalry with my father and sex with my mother.

5.

During the winter term I recovered my equanimity, partly through acting a small part in a production of *Henry IV, Part 2,* directed by Peter Wood for the Marlowe Society. When it was over I could hardly wait for the month-long Easter vacation in order to give myself a change of scene and carry out at least a symbolic flight from my feeling of entrapment. I took a train to Cornwall and set out to pedal my way up the west of England on an ancient bicycle, hitchhiking on trucks or resorting to trains when the weather got too bad. There are times when escape is the right solution, and this was one of them. In the damp chill of late March and early April, as the leaves began to come out, I pumped along the back roads of Devon and Somerset, Gloucestershire, Worcestershire, Shropshire, and Westmoreland. I slept in hostels, rooming houses, and haystacks; I drank pints of ale or rough cider in pubs and ate fried fish or bread and cheese. For the first time since leaving Colorado five years earlier I found myself exposed to open countryside. I had not suspected how much I had missed it. I flourished on the exercise in the free air. For those weeks, almost alone in my fourteen months of *Wanderjahr,* my journals can be read without embarrassment. The open country, the cuckoos and daffodils, the fields of bean poles and corn, the sheep in their pastures, names like Glastonbury and Ludlow, awakened me to my own

language, a natural American speech rhythm that neither
Harvard nor Cambridge had taught me, and that was certainly not my father's:

A good dinner and then back to "The Jolly Sailor" for an hour
or so. Conversation: Newmarket, the Grand National, an Irish-
man who ran off with a girl in a fishing boat, registration of
somebody's new boat, what Harry X said in the mackerel shed
this morning that might cause ructions in the family, and what
about his wife coming home at two or three o'clock last week?
Maybe she was working somewhere. "The bloody bugger doan't
know when to open 'is mouth. Somebody ought to tell 'um."
"Won't be 'is woife. Can't tell she nothing." "Well, what does
'er want 'anging around wi' that bloody Jim fer?" "Naow, naow,
'er moight ev been working theer."
Types: (1) Talkative old geezer, few teeth, seamed face, black
turtleneck, battered hat, suspicious about Harry. (2) Straight
little chap with cap. Honest open face, repetitive but inclined
to think the best of Harry. (3) Little old chap with walrus
moustache, pipe, and tidy hat, reserves judgment about Harry,
only waiting for domino game to start. (4) Talkative young
man without hat waiting to go out with his girl. Respected on
racing, ignored on fishery subjects. (5) Sharp-eyed man with
stand-up collar and mousy moustache, obviously a tradesman,
unlike the others. Very Respectable. Talked almost like Vermont.
A little overfriendly and voluble, tolerated but not respected.
(6) A fat, peak-capped, overalled garageman, profane, jolly, and
bibulous. I drank sweet cider and kept my peace.
About ten, up and away towards Bideford, stopping for a drink
at a nice old pub, with dozens of pictures of Churchill. On into
Bideford, a steep-streeted market town not unattractive. A drink
at an old pub undergoing repair, and lunch for 1s. 6d. at the
British Restaurant. After down off along the river & basked on
the sand for half an hour or so. Thence off toward Barnstaple,
stopped along the way at a filling station, where the toilet paper
was a review from last September's *Daily Mirror* of J. B. Priestley's

Delight. Favorable. Flat and dullish country into Barnstaple, where stopped for an ice cream and heard the broadcast of the Grand National, speculation on the outcome of which has been the main item of pub conversation all the way. The favorite won. Out of Barnstaple up into lovely hills, covered with hundreds of sheep, new lambs capering, horsemen in the lanes, sun bright, all very pretty, but hard & tiring going. Sheep pastures gave way to woods after a time, mostly beeches, their leaves not yet out. Few flowers here—some daffodils occasionally. Stopped at a hotel late in afternoon for a half-pint, & a puddingy N. Devon jokester, after a little conversation & inquiry, wanted to know if I was going to pull out my six-guns & shoot up the place. I should have asked him where he left his butter.

It felt marvelous to be able to write simply and spontaneously and not to think of my parents as an audience. I began to gain hope that I might someday be able to speak in my own voice, now that I could survey my father's country without having to speak in his. I celebrated by writing a little book of illustrated clerihews and sent it for my parents' silver wedding anniversary as a peace offering.

When I returned to Cambridge I was ready for the most idyllic May and June of my life, the glory of the English spring. I now gladly gave myself to the pleasures of the university, feeling for once that I had something to give in return. As Cambridge unfolded into flower, I seemed to open up with it. The peak came on a picnic on the banks of the Granta on a daisy-and-buttercup day in June. I had punted a skiff, containing mainly girls and beer, upriver to moor it in the Grantchester meadows for swimming. A cuckoo was still singing—hoarsely, for it was the end of his season—from a thicket nearby. Seven of us lay in the sun and smiled. I sat cross-legged in front of Elizabeth, a ruddy, warm-hearted milkmaid of a girl with the lavish body of a woman and the quick generous eyes of a child. We made each other daisy chains, and I looped one in her hair. A droplet of sweat ambled from her forehead down the side of her nose. When she tipped her head back to laugh, it turned into a jewel. I reached out to wipe it away and touched her warm skin. We were suffused with a sensuousness as vivid as the paintings of Renoir's women. The body of the girl, the fat green grass, the throaty cry of the cuckoo, held the trickle of spring, the pulse of stirring blood. Somewhere in me that afternoon has never stopped happening.

By the time the Cambridge year finished, I had been offered, and had accepted, an editorial job in New York. I spent the summer saying farewell to Europe, visiting friends in Paris, and scuttling from café to café to gather the news when war broke out in Korea. I visited more of my father's middle-aged friends among the enclaves of the Pax Americana—a general in Brussels ("Buck" Lanham, said to be the model for Hemingway's Colonel Cantwell); a German-American captain in Regensburg who took me deer hunting in the hills; Howard and Bessie Jones at the Amerika-institut in Munich. Then I returned to England.

On my last visit to Priestley's house in the Isle of Wight, I had more to give than on my earlier visits. Now I came in my own right and not as my father's son only. I had learned the way around England, including much about the country that my father had never known, and I had discovered to my relief that it had a present tense as well as a past perfect. Priestley's spirit, the fires that lay banked in his jowly stumpy body, behind his lidded eyes and the rising clouds of pipe smoke and the thick rumble of his Yorkshire accent, finally responded not to my Harvard glibness but to the tug and flicker of my acceptance of the pleasures and the smoldering vitality of England. Our friendship really began here—our friendship for each other as opposed to our common cause with my father—and would continue as long as we lived.

There was an enormous distance between Priestley's image and his self, between his persona and his anima, as there was, I discovered later, with Robert Frost. Both men seemed simpler on the surface than they were within. Frost was witty, while Priestley was comic. Priestley was unwary, even reckless, about showing anger. Like Frost he believed, and practiced his belief, that language could be kept simple and translucent without betraying the depths beneath it, but he chose to scatter himself broadly, out of a prose writer's impatience, rather than keep himself supple and light-footed by the strict exercise of bringing things up to the surface from very deep. He considered himself (wrongly, I think) a poet, but he was industrious and could not bear not to write. A poet must know when not to put pen to paper.*

I began to say my London good-byes. Ten days before I was to sail I walked into a pub in Saint Martin's Lane and saw Elizabeth sitting at a table with some friends. The sight of her lit me like a lamp, and within minutes this accidental meeting seemed to have been inevitable. I had learned by now that she was unhappily married and that she wanted to divorce her husband but keep her child. Though I was frightened of the implications of her need and was, I knew, years away from marriage, I could not deny the joy we instantly discovered in each other, nor this time did I try to resist it.

---

* Both Frost and Priestley have been much misunderstood, and both have given cause for misunderstanding. Once I brought the two together, the only time the two men met. They misunderstood each other to the bone. Priestley said, "What a sweet old man." Frost said, "I was glad to meet your friend the socialist."

The group left the pub and took a bus to the East End of London for some supper. On the way Elizabeth and I, sitting together, became so intensely conscious of each other that we could no longer bear the constraint of company. As soon as we arrived at the end of the line we stole away from our friends, got back on the bus, and rode and rambled to the nearest place we could find to be alone, the dark lawns of St. James's Park, where we lay together and asked, "When did you first know?" Later that night we found a room together. I loved her and trusted her because she was like a child. She taught me that love could convey joy.

We spent three nights together before I sailed. When we were not lying abed, we walked around London and sang each other airs from *The Beggar's Opera*. Everything was made keener between us, open to both tears and laughter, because my departure was so close at hand and she was so unhappy in her marriage. On August 16, 1950, the day after the princess Anne was born, I sailed for New York, and we have never seen each other again. Though she wrote me twice, I never answered. I talked about Elizabeth to my mother, who harshly advised me not to reply. It was all the encouragement I needed to reject love so soon after discovering it. Maybe my mother's youthful experience with the playwright caused her to be so disapproving—or else the reality of her middle age had made her bitter about the reliability of sudden romance. More likely, however, she was simply jealous, and I, eager for an excuse to deny my inconvenient emotions, played into her hands. In any case, Elizabeth got her divorce, and I did nothing.

I had arrived in New York on the old *Queen Elizabeth,* having slept my way through part of a hurricane, with scars healed, my body and mind my own as they had not been when I left, wounded and seeking shelter, the summer before. I had been blooded during my absence, I had gone deeper into both strength and weakness, and now my formal education was over. I was ready to be tested by the "real world," but I was still far from understanding that the real world does not work by competitive examination.

Part Two

IV

The Ropewalk

Look at my face, never an honest one.
It covers my desertion by pretending
That words have never meant a thing to me.
This face settles for the lie.

P.D., "The Deserted Poet"

As the years pass, I take greater pleasure
In boasting where I found heart's-ease,
Forget-me-not, all the pretty creatures
That yearned so ardently from their dewy beds.

P.D., "The Collector"

1.

My adult self—what I had uncovered of it in England—did not stay exposed to the air long. Once I had denied Elizabeth, other backslidings were easy. The progress of the Korean War made it fairly clear that I would be drafted soon, so why go to all the trouble of finding a place of my own to live? Just before my arrival in New York my father had found a promising job on the administrative staff of Hunter College, and my parents rented an apartment, with a spare room for me, on East Fifty-seventh Street. I moved in and helped them arrange the furniture and alphabetize the books. It was a comfortable, convenient apartment on the sixteenth floor, with (in those days) a good clear view south over Manhattan to the Chrysler Building. Our familiar furniture, the paintings, the piano, all slipped easily into place. It seemed strange to have to use an elevator to get to the ground, but, once there, I could walk through the city streets to my new job on Madison Avenue. It was as though my father and I were beginning over together.

I devoted the next six months, obsessively, to learning my trade. I did not even try to work out a new relationship with my family, but pretended that I was only once again on vacation from school. This postponement seems to me in retrospect one of the worst mistakes I ever made, for it led to further postponements that lasted almost ten years. Yet at the time I seemed to have no choice.

My new career was book publishing. I did not precisely choose it, but it was one of those arranged marriages that turn out happily. My background suited it. Back in Colorado the high season of our family year had always been late July and early August, when the University of Colorado sponsored the Writers' Conference, of which my father was the director. My mother, his associate, traveled to New York for several weeks every spring to recruit staff and arrange publicity. Preparations started as soon as ordinary classes ceased in June, rising to a fever when the writers arrived.

All through my childhood years, from seven to thirteen, I had watched the writers come and go as though they were a breed apart. I acted as my father's messenger to these fabled creatures, running anxious errands on my bicycle to deliver manuscripts that must not be spilled or lost. As I grew older I occasionally sat at the back of the workshop sessions and listened. When my parents gave parties for the writers I looked forward to seeing them come through our door, and like a boy in a storybook I lurked at the top of the stairs after I should have been in bed and listened to the gaiety below. The zest drawn from those mysterious regions east of the Great Plains, where writers almost always seemed to come from, lit up my mother and father with excitement.

Except for Robert Frost and my athletic hero Red Warren, none of the writers made a greater impression on me than Ford Madox Ford, who wheezed slowly up our front walk one afternoon in 1937 or 1938, with an imperially gouty foot swathed in bandages, and leaning on the arm of his fourth wife, Janice Biala. Late in his stay with us he commandeered the kitchen for a whole day and perched on a stool to instruct Biala and other helpers in the preparation of a famous recipe for mock venison, based on marinated mutton. No real venison I have ever eaten lived up to Ford's imitation, just as real life had a way of never living up to his accounts of it. He gave a public lecture that summer, since celebrated in a poem of Robert Lowell's, on the subject of his notorious collaboration with Joseph Conrad. A capacity crowd turned out. The lecture went on an hour and a half; but the combination of gout, asthma, and altitude so reduced Ford's vocal powers, and his murmuring head bowed so low over his text, that the audience gave up and crept away without his realizing it. When at last he lifted his head barely a dozen stalwarts remained.

Carl Sandburg came and went over a period of years, always accompanied by his guitar and his stogy. He spent one visit reading proofs of his *Lincoln: The War Years,* a task he performed outdoors on a canvas chair, wearing a green eyeshade. Whenever he passed me on the stairs, he would chortle horribly and chant the lines of some song, "Peter Peter Peter Peter Peter over the sea. . . ." I found his joke unfathomable.

Paul Horgan, Witter Bynner, and Eric Knight were all among the favorites of us children, as of my parents. Bynner's deep laugh was an entertainment in itself, and we would sit in suspense on the sofa and wait for it to erupt. Eric Knight told us snatches of stories about Sam Small, the Flying Yorkshireman; and we watched him yearningly because he had written *Lassie Come-Home,* one of our favorite books. Paul Horgan performed wonderful entertainments, like making pen-and-ink sketches of mythical writers, or playing the overture to *Tannhäuser* on our piano with a whisk broom or an orange.

Ralph Hodgson, a small, very old, mysterious poet with a face like a hound's, smoked tiny cherry wood pipes. He would fill eight or ten at a time, in advance, and lay them out in rows on a table in front of him. When this chore was done he would hold very grave conversations with my sister Lesley and me, asking us questions but, unlike most adults, listening to our answers.

In contrast to these colorful folk, John Crowe Ransom, now one of my favorite poets, made no impression on me at all, though I believe he may have been present when I first identified the red-winged blackbird on a car ride. Or was that John Peale Bishop, the one with the moustache? I got them mixed up because they both had three names.

How trivial such memories are, and yet they are all it takes to set up a pantheon. Had I been brought up in Grosse Pointe or Cos Cob I might have venerated auto magnates or bankers—but to my parents writers occupied a special, a senatorial rank in society, and our house was simply consecrated to their service for that brief period each summer.

At Harvard I had felt vaguely tempted by the law, but I could hardly ignore the tug of my family's chronic attraction to writers as friends, even less the awe which shrouded my father's dedication to words and the sound of words. During my year abroad at Cambridge my father heard from Denver Lindley, the translator and editor at Harcourt, Brace, who had been among those I consulted a year or two earlier. He reported that a beginning editorial position would be vacant at Harcourt in the autumn. Would I be interested? Teddie wrote me at once, clearly excited. I had not planned to seek a job in publishing, but I couldn't imagine not being interested, and my father thought it a wonderful opportunity. I wrote a carefully phrased letter of application and, after a perfunctory interview by a Harcourt vice-president at the Savoy Hotel, London, in early June, the job was mine, the marriage was arranged. I had been spared another choice.

2.

The earliest days of a job are the ones we remember best. Everything is new then, and we inefficiently remember what later we train ourselves to forget. In September 1950 I was shown to a gray cubicle in the Harcourt, Brace offices, surrounded by shelves of shoulder height. It contained two desks, one of which was to be mine. The shelves were filled with unread manuscripts. I was to read them and write reports on their suitability for publication. Then I was left to myself. I read myself dizzy. I had no idea that so many manuscripts could have been perpetrated, nor such bad ones.

For the next six months I spent every day in a daze of typewritten reading. Nobody who has not worked as an editor realizes how much time the profession devotes to the unprinted word. My average consumption fell between fifteen and twenty book-length typescripts a week. I seldom read less than a hundred pages of any of these, and I read every word of at least several. My manuscripts were those which had come to the firm without any endorsement, even from a creative writing teacher or a literary agent or one of the firm's authors or an acquaintance of one of the editors. As the most junior editor I read all of them and rejected the hopeless ones, passing on to my seniors those which held any promise at all. Only one of the hundreds of unsolicited manuscripts I read in three years was in fact published by Harcourt, Brace. I also, as junior member, was charged with the chore of keeping track of what the other editors were reading and with nudging them if they dawdled.

The editorial meetings were presided over by Eugene Reynal, the trade publisher who had hired me in London. He was a man of wealth and flair, moon-faced, husky-voiced, given to double-breasted suits, suede shoes, and to crushing out monogrammed cigarettes, after a few puffs, on his office carpet with his heel. The editor in chief was Robert Giroux, prematurely gray, grinning, bland, guarded, enigmatic, an adept at the intrigues of the New York literary scene, and a devoted publisher. My dignified and learned friend Denver Lindley, who read French and German as well as ancient Greek, was a letter writer of great suavity and wit, and the sometime translator of Thomas Mann, Herman Hesse, and Erich Maria Remarque. Alfred Kazin, the firm's literary adviser, arrived at editorial meetings voluble in his discoveries of new Czech writers, of Italians and Israelis, of American writers and critics.

When I went to work, Harcourt, Brace had one of the most impressive general lists of books in America. Founded in 1918 on a base that included the major writers of the Bloomsbury Group and Americans like Sinclair Lewis and Carl Sandburg, the firm between 1950 and my departure in 1955 issued works by virtually every major writer in the English language, from E. M. Forster to John Berryman, from T. S. Eliot to Robert Lowell. The trade list positively embarrassed with its riches, and the editors who served as its custodians struck me as an immensely gifted group who, despite the marvels of their backlist, went on to discover and launch new fiction writers, poets, and critics like Flannery O'Connor, Randall Jarrell, and Hannah Arendt. To work with such editors and read such manuscripts struck me as the luckiest sort of work in the world.

3.

My five years in New York were interrupted but not ultimately altered by a two-year absence in the Army. I was
drafted while the Korean War was still at its height, on
March 5, 1951, and was discharged two years later on the day
after Stalin's death. I was soon crawling on elbows and knees
over the frozen dirt of Fort Devens, Massachusetts, undergoing basic infantry training with the 278th Regimental
Combat Team, a reserve unit of the Tennessee National
Guard. Throughout the cold New England spring I learned
to do without sleep, to keep my shoes as shiny as a mirror and
my rifle barrel cleaner than my teeth. I saw more reason to
take pride in basic training than in any previous test. I was a
year or two older than most of the other draftees and better
used to being away from home. I took to the physical rigors
and the implied competition as naturally as if I had enlisted.
I soon became an acting squad leader, counting cadence and
marching groups of men from place to place.

I came to know the sandy soil and the bilious cream-yellow
barracks of Fort Devens with an intimacy of the flesh. When
your elbows bear the impression of the pebbles in the ground
and when you have flicked its dust off your shoe soles with a
toothbrush at night; when you have lain on a hillside in cold
and snow and rain and scrabbled little heaps of dirt and pine
needles around the edges of your blanket roll for insulation;
when the bullets your rifle fires kick up a spray of sand at two
hundred yards' distance from the chilblained finger you have
just squeezed on its trigger; when your hands blister from
digging trenches in hard clay with a tiny portable spade and
filling them up again; when you have marched, or double-
timed, twenty miles across scrubby sandhills and waded the

sluggish swamps, you know more about that place than other places. I became as comfortable on the hard ground and the asphalt parking lots of Fort Devens as on any mattress, and I even learned to catch ten-minute naps with my head pillowed on a steel helmet.

The most satisfying thing about the Army was being exposed to American male talk, with the ruffles and flourishes of profanity that decorated it. Tennesseans, like most American Southerners, are blessed with an effortless access to the rhythm of our language that my Easterly education had left out. I smiled to listen to the cooks swearing at one another as I washed huge greasy aluminum kettles on KP; I relished the ingenuity of rodomontade with which First Sergeant Smith could excoriate a helplessly admiring company of recruits standing at attention. I learned how hardship is converted into humor, how the words of one's tongue relate to the aching muscles of one's body. The pleasure of coming in from two cold hours on guard duty at four in the morning and cursing your condition while creaking into bed for a short sleep is nothing to be scorned. So long as the Army was physical, I actually enjoyed it.

Towards the end of basic training we began to repeat the easy training with machine guns and recoilless rifles that we had already learned. The first sergeant one day asked for volunteers to do some typing. I was bored so I raised my hand. I shortly found myself reassigned to a quartermaster depot where I typed out invoices all day long. ("6 pr. shoes, brown, low quarter, 9 B. 12 ea. rifles, .30 cal, M-1, w. sling.") Several weeks of this tried one's patience and dignity far more than crawling in the dirt had done. I wrote to my father suggesting that he pull one of his old Army strings to get me transferred to a more "useful" assignment, and so it was that instead of going to Korea in a supply depot or an infantry company I spent the next twenty months at various American Army posts as part of a bizarre little unit called the Second Loudspeaker and Leaflet Company.

The 2nd L & L was stationed at first at Fort Riley, Kansas, the old frontier cavalry post. The towns nearby, Manhattan and Junction City, were still crippled by the terrible 1951 flood of the Kansas River, which had filled basements with stinking mud. The summer heat of the Great Plains had not been postponed on that account. We sweltered in hundred-degree steam. My record had preceded me (Oh, that I had never confessed my acquaintance with a typewriter!), and I was promptly appointed assistant company clerk and "acting corporal." For the next six months I was responsible for keeping all the company's official records, beginning each day with the Morning Report, which itemized every official transaction, every transfer, every promotion or demotion or disciplinary action, every leave, every set of orders or movement of the company. The Morning Report must be compiled with scrupulous accuracy: not only might there be no typing mistakes, but no erasures were allowed. Even if I got up at 5 A.M. I might have to type the thing fifteen times before getting it right. Nor might it be written in English. Our lingua franca was military jargon: "EM: Sgt Spezze, Paul, ER31100574, trans HQ Gen Ad 1106 Svc Com per DOD 4967, AR 456, 5A Dir dtd 23 Nov 51."

In addition to this clerical penance, the company commander mustered me into service as a training lecturer. The Second Loudspeaker and Leaflet Company's "mission" was to prepare itself to conduct "tactical psychological warfare (psywar) operations at Army Headquarters Level." This meant in plain but wordier English that our company of 124 men, equipped with portable printing presses in vans, would bring to bear the talents of linguists and propagandists on the enemy in battle. We were to print and disseminate leaflets and broadcast loudspeaker appeals in attempts to undermine the enemy's morale and get him to surrender. Unfortunately nobody knows how to do this.

Moreover, it is impossible to practice propaganda without an audience. The 2nd L & L was stationed "in reserve" in the United States in case the 1st L & L (Korea) or the 5th L & L (Germany) were to be wiped out. Whose morale were we supposed to undermine? Army Personnel kept sending us all-purpose bodies to train: illiterate Lithuanian refugees, Tagalog peasants with filed teeth who had enlisted in the U.S. Army to escape Philippine village life, Ukrainian carpenters, White Russian mechanics, Nisei from Hawaii, cooks from Louisiana, advertising copywriters from New York, commercial artists from Omaha, and a group of colorful German-American photolithographers from Milwaukee who ran the printing presses when there was anything to print. The only group who had any real work to do were the Nisei, who made themselves masters of the supply room and piled up vast resources of goods and money which they invested with inexorable success in juggernaut payday poker games.

Nobody in the Army knew what to do with us. Our company commander was a handsome easygoing All-American lady-killer, who seldom ventured forth by daylight, for the sake of his hung-over eyesight. The executive officer was an advertising type from Chicago who babbled and chirped when he wasn't needed but vanished when questions were asked or orders were called for. Everyone knows that first sergeants actually run the Army. Ours was a bewildered middle-aged former supply sergeant named Huggins, who hadn't the faintest idea what psychological warfare might be, but kept his officers out of trouble and his men in reasonably presentable condition.

As company clerk I became adept at the regulations, but this did not help me when I had to deal with the men. I had no natural authority whatever. One day a squad of men infuriated me by refusing to keep quiet in ranks, so I kept marching them up and down to make them shut up. When I finally halted them, the men—all of them barracks mates and some almost friends—broke ranks and walked away without looking back. I was not stupid enough to follow up their disobedience, but I spent a sleepless night absorbing the lesson that authority is dependent on the consent of the subordinate.

I read the two or three books that summarized World War II's lessons on the subject of psychological warfare. The Army provided dozens of mimeographed lecture outlines cribbed from the books. Two officers and I alternated in lecturing the poor bored Ukrainians and Filipinos for several hours a day on the distinctions between black, white, and gray propaganda, on the "optimum utilization of local conditions," on the importance of telling credible lies if you could not tell the truth. I began to learn something about teaching and about what made people willing to learn. Though I was an impatient teacher, I managed with a certain combination of tolerance and irony to keep both myself and the class clear of total boredom, while treating the Army's offering with a healthy skepticism.

My instructional work managed to free me from the dreaded job of company clerk, and I was glad to pay the price of resuming guard duty and KP. Manual work, even make-work, is better than bureaucratic minuets. The company commander gave me the title of "acting chief script writer." We killed hours every day listening to the English-language news on Radio Moscow—"monitoring," it was called, for "content analysis." We compared the American newspaper reports on Korean military action with Moscow's. This was meant to instruct us in the duplicity and bias of Moscow's propaganda, but it also made us increasingly aware of the bias in American news reporting.

The days in Kansas were pretty dull, and the nights were not much better. Yet southern Kansas at the time was larded with Army and Air Force bases, and on weekends when we had saved our pay we might make sallies toward Topeka in search of whiskey and wild, wild women. In Kansas women were often easier to find than whiskey. Salina in particular was full of girls, lonely wives and fiancées of absent soldiers and airmen, or free agents who spent their evenings dancing and drinking and going to bed with whatever soldier pleased them most in the crowd at the bar. If by bad luck the amateurs were outnumbered after payday, whorehouses took care of the overflow.

On a Saturday afternoon three or four of us would pile into someone's car and drive to the outskirts of Salina and a few beer halls where couples danced to the jukebox and ate hamburgers and French fries. Hard liquor could not be sold at the bar, but customers could bring a bottle of whiskey, genteelly inserted in a paper bag, and order "set-ups," ginger ale or Seven-Up or Dr Pepper or Coke. We grinned at each other in the din, assured that we were having the time of our lives, and leered at the girls. If anyone reached an understanding on the dance floor, he simply borrowed the car and drove out of town to some dark wheat field. When he returned, his companions smirked, and the girl pretended not to notice.

At first I enjoyed these expeditions hugely. The very clangor and coarseness of the entertainment had its own vitality. One night in Salina, when a musty, sulky girl pressed herself against me on the dance floor, it was I who borrowed the car and drove into the dark. I pulled off the road into a field and turned off the lights, and she slid under me before I touched her, quick as a cat. It was over in a minute or two, and as I muzzily recovered I realized that the girl had been transformed—not by the act, but by its being over. On the way back to the bar she prattled and prated as cozily as if we had known each other for years. The moment we entered the bar she resumed her moody silence and stalked away without looking back. I returned to my table and tried to look knowing. We had all performed as expected. It was the American way.

I had no idea what dangerous ground I was walking. The postponement of a year before was about to demand payment. When I had gone to work in New York, living in my parents' apartment, I had wound myself into a cocoon so thick that all the emotions that had been freed at last in Europe were forced to lie dormant. While they lay they gathered new strength, and as the months went by they began tensing for their time to come. I had walked through my months in New York like a zombie, given over by day and night to books and manuscripts while I waited, dangling, for my draft call to come. Then, in the early spring, I had been plunged into basic training, invigorating, mindless, competitive. Not till I was transferred to Kansas and the sedentary routines of barracks life did I begin to feel myself again. And then what? Dressed in a little authority, I began to doubt whether I deserved it; I went out with the boys, trying to rival them in drinking whiskey and chasing tail. It was a pretty good act, but nobody believed in it.

Reveille formations, polished shoes and neatly crisscrossed shoelaces, orientation lectures on the menace of communism, the rigid order of the Morning Report on the one hand; the squalors of Salina Saturday nights, the rich obscenities of barracks talk, the long Kansas highways on the other—neither role gave any play to the feminine part of my nature. Only in letters written to friends—I did not entrust my parents with the soulful letters I wrote to friends as far away as Europe—did I intimate that there was any more to me than the acting corporal.

When my emotions burst from hiding at last they were those of a stranger, violent with self-hate. I set off, one Friday morning, on a three-day pass. I bought a Greyhound bus ticket to Colorado to revisit the scenes of my childhood, but something stopped me from going so far, a kind of dread. As I rode the bus toward Manhattan, Kansas, with the long lime-stone hills outside the window, I felt as though I were changing into someone else. I got off in a panic in Manhattan and checked into a hotel room to hide. I had with me a copy of *Boswell's London Journal,* and I began to read, but I soon put the book away. Boswell's self-regard, his innumerable cases of clap and the self-medications he undertook aroused nothing but further revulsion for the splashings and mud-dlings I had been indulging in. The child in me, who had wanted to cross the water to reach his mother on the other side, had turned into a Caliban. I felt a prisoner of a grosser self; I could not breathe. I sank into a state that was neither conscious nor unconscious. For two nights and a day, I left my hotel room only once for a meal, and lay the rest of the time staring at the barred patterns of the wallpaper like a prisoner, running my fingers over the cotton tufts on the counterpane as I had on my childhood bed.

Before dawn on the Sunday morning I finally and desper-ately knew myself a sinner, but this flash also brought with it an intimation of Grace. My mind lightened. The sun rose. I began to hear words that lifted me as in Elijah's chariot. They were the cadences of my father's voice. The voices I heard were those of poetry, but I thought they were the Voice of God.

> God's most deep decree
> Bitter would have me taste. The taste was me.

> No, worst, there is none. Pitched past pitch of grief . . .

> And as I raged and grew more fierce and wild
>   At every word,
> Methought I heard one calling, Child,
>   And I replied, My Lord.

I got up and left the hotel, looking for something. In the sunshine of the main street I came to a funeral parlor which carried the sign: "Episcopal Church Services Will Be Held Here Until Flood Damage To Church Is Repaired. Morning Prayer: 10:30." I went in and sat on one of the folding chairs. Other people entered, and soon I heard my voice saying with the others:

Almighty God, Father of our Lord Jesus Christ, Maker of all things, Judge of all men; We acknowledge and bewail our manifold sins and wickedness, Which we from time to time most grievously have committed, By thought, word, and deed, against thy Divine Majesty, Provoking most justly thy wrath and indignation against us. We do earnestly repent, And are heartily sorry for these our misdoings: The remembrance of them is grievous unto us; The burden of them is intolerable. . . .

I was home again, a baby in the room with my father's voice and near my mother's breast. That was the peace that passed understanding.

The service ended. I filed out with the others and shook the minister's hand. A woman came up to me in my uniform. She was middle-aged. Her spectacles gleamed. Her hands were bandaged: eczema, not stigmata. Would the soldier come to dinner with her and her family? There was roast chicken, carved by the father, a professor of entomology, an expert in insect-resistant crops. There was a pale daughter, a weedy son. We talked of the church, of the service, of the sacraments.

The next week I went to the Episcopal church in Junction City, joined the choir, and undertook instruction for baptism and confirmation. It had been the work of one day to decide that I wanted to become an Anglican. Judaism? Catholicism? No. It was the *English* language I needed, and the singing and chanting loomed as importantly as the spoken ritual. The following months were a moil of discovery and rediscovery. I took up piano lessons again with the church organist. I committed the articles and creeds of the church to memory. When my task was done I knelt before the minister, a former railroad timekeeper, and confessed all my sins aloud. The next morning I was baptized; the next week, confirmed by the Bishop of Eastern Kansas. The entomology professor and his wife were my godparents. My mother and father received a letter marveling at the firm voice in which I had uttered the responses. I wrote long, sanctimonious, embarrassing letters home full of churchly goo.

My poor parents never knew what to make of all this. By the time I was discharged from the Army eighteen months later I was hard put to explain it myself. But while the all-male leveling of the Army went on, the church served as the holy goblet of poetry and music, the two sacred influences that my parents had endowed me with. "When all things began, the Word already was. The Word dwelt with God, and what God was, the Word was. . . . The light shines on in the dark and the darkness has never mastered it." It is one of those great tautologies which have the magical capacity to increase in truth the more often they are encountered. For me the Word was embodied in poetry and music: I have never ceased to regard them as gifts beyond human understanding. I had found my way back to my inner life, but, after I left the Army, I proved no exception to the rule that intellectuals make untrustworthy converts.

In spite of my exaltation, barracks life went on and on, winding down into boredom, to disillusion, disgust, and even cynicism. Our Kansas training program was followed by maneuvers in Texas. We dropped leaflets on the "aggressor forces" at Fort Hood, warning them that there were rattlesnakes coiled in the mesquite, and tempting them to surrender to sexy loudspeaker appeals from a nubile WAC. Then the 2nd L & L moved to North Carolina, where the Army set up a Psychological Warfare Center at Fort Bragg, in conjunction with its new Special Forces Headquarters. I began to spend weekends in the congenial surroundings of Chapel Hill and Durham and went to church less regularly. A cog slipped at the Pentagon, and the Center took delivery of some forty lieutenant colonels and colonels, more than enough to staff an entire infantry division of ten thousand men. Each colonel demanded a jeep driver, a clerk-typist, an orderly, and, if feasible, a staff. The officers' mess drafted us, contrary to regulations, to wait on their tables and wash their pots. We stood guard duty and carried out housekeeping details, and our little band of four hundred men melted away from their presses and microphones like summer snowbanks. We labored in the seasonal heat, and at night played cards and drank beer.

As the Korean War wound down, our little "Psywar" enclave wound down with it, though the colonels continued to multiply like milkweed. We began to suspect that "Psywar" had become the elephants' graveyard, that the Army was sending all those colonels to Fort Bragg to keep them from killing anyone. I was assigned for several months—I can no longer remember why—to do research on Albania's vulnerability to psychological warfare. I read books in the Psywar library and CIA reports. The rest of the team was discharged from the service before we could finish our paper, and I wrote the report alone. It was stamped SECRET and sent to Washington, where nobody ever read it. Next I was put in charge of a crew of black soldiers to stoke the furnaces in our part of the camp (the Army was officially desegregated, but all the stokers were black except me, and I was the NCO), and for the last month or so of my Army duty I slept by day and wandered the camp at night, checking on the furnaces or reading Proust and Joyce Cary in between making sure that the colonels kept warm. I got to be quite expert in the quirks of furnaces fired with Appalachian coal. To have learned that was to have learned something.

4.

In the ten years before my discharge I had never lived anywhere for more than nine months at a stretch. I wanted my new place to be both "home," and "mine," that is to serve purposes that so far my experience had proved contradictory. To strike a balance between dependence and loneliness, I arranged, even before leaving the Army, that my sister and I should share our living quarters. It was an unusual step, motivated by the same spirit that had drawn us to make music together years before, a mixture of defiance and timidity. Lesley had graduated from college and was working as a copyeditor at G. P. Putnam's, the publishing firm. With regard to our parents we were in the same boat, attracted yet repelled by powerful forces. I rationalized my impulse to nest with my sister by telling myself I was rescuing her from the Family Situation. The apartment we took in New York, in a brownstone house on East Thirty-eighth Street near the Third Avenue "El," would shelter me for over two years.

It was a charming little place, two bed-sitting-rooms on the same floor, front and back, with two bathrooms, one of which had been enlarged into a tiny kitchen. The lower floors of the house were used, during the daytime only, by our landlord's documentary film company. We invited friends and parents alike to meals, for which I developed an interesting repertoire of Chinese cookery. With our own phone and our own address, we tolerated each other with a mixture of familiar affection and disapproving exasperation. Why, I wondered, couldn't my sister be more like *me?* Lord knows she was trying—to her cost. Her publishing job didn't suit her, but I had gone into publishing, and she was trying to follow my example if it killed her. She wondered why I chased girls so unremittingly: it made her nervous. Lesley went off to England after a year. There she made her own discoveries about the fatherland and studied the guitar so that she could perform the witty satirical songs she was beginning to compose. By roundabout routes we would both eventually come to the making of verses.

For me that day was far off. Back in New York, I hungered to write and tried every device to keep myself at it. I kept journals, but they sputtered out. I began short stories on a flood of inspiration but never finished them. Occasionally, with a feeling of awe, I tried my hand at a poem, but I always treated it as an exercise, a puzzle that must be completed at one sitting or discarded. Folders of unfinished written material began to accumulate, but I had no capacity to press beyond the first flush of excitement. I started three novels but never got as far as a second chapter. I did write a few book reviews for *The New Leader,* on the invitation of an editor whom I met at a party.

I hurled myself into editorial work, however, with an unnatural, even a self-defeating intensity which gave me the most reliable of excuses for doing nothing else: *no time.* It took me only a matter of weeks after my return from the Army to become immersed in reading manuscripts again. Three or four times a year I traveled through New England selling Harcourt, Brace's list of books to stores and looking for new authors among the colleges. I kept learning more about publishing, but the pleasures of increasing competence were not enough. I had had my warnings in England and Kansas. I knew that something was miserably wrong, and that sooner or later I would have to change my life.

My incapacity to write infected everything I did. It drove me to overwork, it spurred me into a breathless, unrelenting pursuit of girls, which, natural enough in itself, became unnaturally transformed into a kind of flight. The sensitivity which I was not willing to acknowledge in myself became contorted into a tool, even a weapon. The girls I met at New York parties affected a worldliness which presented a challenge to know them by having them. None of us emigrants from the American West to the big city could wholly shake off a secret conviction that among the sophisticates we could never be anything but yokels, that the arenas of cocktail parties had to be traversed with all the wary formality of toreros. The principal aim of getting one of these girls naked into bed was to make her a child like myself, to become her equal for an hour even though when we got up and dressed we might act as cool as strangers. I believed that through love I could find truth, but in fact I was looking for neither. Few of the girls I pursued in these years even became my friends.

I developed a sixth sense about whether a girl was attracted to me and often found myself paying court to a girl "who did not please me, who was not my style," simply because I sensed that *I* pleased *her*. The fashion of the fifties decreed that a man could be counted a success as a lover only if he gave satisfaction. I could not imagine why my conscientious efforts to give girls pleasure only seemed to make them unhappy. Lines from Eliot's *The Cocktail Party* echoed my frustration:

> To men of a certain type
> The suspicion that they are incapable of loving
> Is as disturbing to their self-esteem
> As, in cruder men, the fear of impotence.

My more frequent form of escape, overwork, adopted an equally conscientious disguise. If I secretly thought of myself as a precocious child, I made every effort to please my superiors as though they were teachers in school. Though this might give them reasonable satisfaction, the harder I worked the deeper the division between my public and private selves grew. I could not seem to remember, no matter how often I had learned it (usually outdoors, in Colorado, on the open roads of England or Italy, or in the Army), that my own identity could be real to me only if I discarded the restraints of the good-student syndrome, and tried to please myself instead of my elders. My deepest instincts, to love and to write, must be repressed as selfish and dangerous simply because they were *me*.

I had been exempted so long from competition by youth, frailty, and illness that I had to pretend to a false strength to affect the determined, acquisitive faces of male editors, businessmen, and all other people who were neither parents, teachers, nor doctors to me. Only a precocity, whose surfaces might imitate the ruggedness of competition, would see me through.

Though strength was what I thought I needed to gain approval, I could not imagine myself being *loved* unless I were as weak as a child. For the time being all I dared flaunt in public was my quick, ingenious, pace-setting, "male" side. I kept my intuitive, female side secret, reserving it for the privacies of bed talk, for the confessions that pass for conversation between young lovers. This produced as great a distortion as my parading of the masculine. I secretly distrusted one role as much as the other. If persisted in, this could only result in what psychiatrists call illness. While I divided myself arbitrarily into half lives, I had no whole self on which I could base my creative efforts. Every time I began a poem or a fiction it fell apart in my hands.

The pressures of the times reinforced my neurosis. The early fifties in New York were a singular era for the American middle class. An immigration of my contemporaries, more highly trained than ever before and moving to New York on the flood tide of an unexampled prosperity, began to take over the key jobs in the new communications media.

Book publishing was overwhelmed by the young, who, unlike the simple tradesmen of the past, had graduated from Yale or Michigan, had won doctorates or enjoyed fellowships for study abroad. Now they flooded New York to find positions in the establishment. Norman Podhoretz in his autobiography and Richard Poirier in "The War Against the Young" have described how the postwar generation waged its scrimmage for position and security and have intimated what it was we suppressed in ourselves in exchange for "making it."

We could see little alternative to subduing our arts and crafts to the purposes of the big institutions, the universities, and the corporations, just as we could see no alternative to the political stalemate of the cold war or to an economy that was gradually reducing all our talents to imagemaking. Publishers had discovered that books of all kinds could be marketed to the masses if prices were kept low enough; yet they left it to the old-fashioned publishers to find them the books to distribute, since discovering authors was a tricky and expensive process, not susceptible to mass techniques. The publishers also found a vast new market of readers (or buyers) among the postwar millions of children who would soon be flooding the schools. The older men who had taught me my trade did not easily adapt to the new patterns, but younger publishers, brighter or better trained than I, began to use the new techniques of imagemaking to promote and sell new kinds of books, texts, records, graphics, plays, dances, music, and fashions.

Advertising, the all-purpose industry that serviced all the others, gradually tightened its hold on many of the most talented of us, but it took us all years to realize that we were changing into something very different from our original intentions. We had agreed to a bargain that traded spontaneity for expertise. Each of us had foreshadowed it when we yielded to the standards of school, college, graduate training, and corporate employment. Yet once the bargain was struck, we began to sense that something was rotten about it. One by one, we found ourselves losing contact with our inner existence. We had begun by wanting to change the world, but we had altered only ourselves. We crept away for a while from the alienations of corporate life, from the imagemakers, from the shrill gabble of cocktail parties and the dark emptiness of the city nights that followed them, to the *agon* of the psychiatrist's couch, our only spiritual luxury. There we searched for what we had mislaid.

In *The Cocktail Party,* the great middle-brow hit of the early fifties, Eliot played shrewdly on two of our most lively symbols—the cocktail party itself and the psychiatrist who mysteriously became its priest. Baffled and somehow dispossessed, many of us turned for succor to a small group of middle-class, technically trained medical men schooled in psychoanalysis, an ingenious art of healing whose philosophical source, strangely, was the nineteenth-century scientific positivism of Helmholtz. It was the only clergy we had left.

5.

In 1955 I was twenty-six, and I realized that nothing had grown or changed in me for years. Though I had developed a certain professional competence in New York, I felt overwhelmed by the city, by its imperatives, its acquisitive pressures, by its compartmentalized and uneasy lovemaking. Though I lived near my parents, I had not learned to live with their adult presence, and I could no longer fittingly play the child. I was keenly aware that I had once again lost the way to myself, and once again the crisis was brought home by a dreamlike confrontation with the elements.

I had taken to chartering, with friends, a tiny boat for day sailing on Little Neck Bay. Once I got the hang of it, I became as interested in sailing as I had once been in mountain climbing. After my sister left New York, my new apartment-mate was Peter Stanford, an experienced transoceanic sailor who had a twenty-three-foot boat of his own, an old Wianno sloop. We planned, for the Memorial Day weekend, a three-day cruise out Long Island Sound, with two girls.

We motored up the East River against tide and current under Hell Gate Bridge and sailed all day to a rendezvous with friends who would come aboard for drinks and supper.

It had been beautifully clear and sunny, warmer than could normally be expected of May. At the Greenwich Yacht Club the banners flew, and the third couple came aboard with a basketful of bottles. We set out across Long Island Sound on a reaching wind. I stood at the front of the cockpit with a beer in my hand and looked ahead toward the Long Island shore. The wind was definitely brisker. The waves were heightening, the troughs were deepening. After a long calm day in the boat I was exhilarated by the jounce of the hull on the wavecaps, the keening of the wind through the rigging, the snowy spume that began to peel off the peaks of the waves.

The others, behind me, were growing gayer and gayer as the boat started to heave and groan, to heel over farther as we made more leeway and had to point up higher into the wind. I sang, pounding the cabin roof to keep time, while the boat reared and curvetted. The wind mounted more and more noisily. Then suddenly, as my excitement reached its height, the boat gathered herself at the top of a wave and buried her nose in the side of the larger one coming after it. The green water sluiced the length of the decks and drenched us all.

Suddenly the color of my day had changed. The sunlight seemed to darken, the song fled from my lips, warmth drained out of my body as if I had been bled. Though the sloop lifted her head to each successive wave, I lost faith that she could do it again or again. This was no longer a game. Under the waters crouched the dark body of death. I felt a helpless but familiar paralysis. We must soon come up against a more formidable wave, and *Whisper* would burrow her nose into its flank, dig deep, founder, and go down. I felt a powerful longing to jump into the sea for silence. I could not abide the pounding of the water, the scouring of the wind, the singing and shouting of the voices behind me. I stumbled below in flight, not sick, not drunk, but frozen. I curled up in the corner of one of the two bunks, clenched myself in the fetal position, wrapped my arms around my head, and tried to lose consciousness. Lying above the keel, my eyes closed, I stayed awake and rigid for hours, but I could not force myself to move a muscle out of my trance of terror.

I heard the sounds of the waves hurling against the hull and the sounds of the others sailing the boat and shouting to each other boozily as we made the last mile into harbor and they prepared supper and the wind died down, but still I could not, did not, move. My girl came below and stroked my brow, thinking me asleep.

Hours later, as we motored after midnight back across the Sound through windless air and pelting rain squalls, I finally roused myself to stir, to stand, to return to life and let the natural motion of the boat carry me ashore. I clambered onto the pier at Greenwich in the same mood of despair and relief that had carried me down from the Crestones. "I will show you fear in a handful of dust." Or in a body of water.

6.

The girl who had accompanied me on the cruise, a divorcée a year or two older than I, had warmed my shrinking capacities for affection. I had given up playing the field. I was grateful for her love and tried to show it, but even after a year I couldn't return the love that was all she wanted. She was a good woman whose first marriage had come to ruin after a baby died, and she needed more certitude than I was yet able to give anybody.

In the meantime, the publishing fortunes of Harcourt, Brace underwent a sudden and to me altogether unexpected change. Every institution has to reckon with the problem of succession. Alfred Harcourt and Donald Brace while alive had never been able to agree on who would govern the corporation after they were gone. During the years while a long-range decision was deferred, the largest minority stockholder, S. Spencer Scott, held the presidency. Harcourt died in 1954 and his son Hastings, who had been passed over, now inherited his father's stock and began jockeying for position. At Christmas it was suddenly announced that William Jovanovich, the thirty-six-year-old executive of the high school publishing division of the company, would become president. In a matter of days Jovanovich had obtained the resignation of Eugene Reynal as head of the general book publishing division and replaced him with John McCallum, a man whose experience outside textbook publishing was nil.

Suddenly every office door was closed. Conspiring staff members huddled together for interminable sessions of anxious gossip. Our minds had been abruptly distracted from the craft of publishing and the curatorship of a fine list to the pursuit of power, the control of the corporation. My colleagues muttered of stock deals and budgets and five-year plans. The authors who had published with the firm began to grow uneasy, for the cooperative camaraderie which had kept the wheels running smoothly gave way to dissension and in due course to resignations.

Robert Giroux went first, having arranged that some of the authors he worked with would accompany him to his new position at Farrar, Straus. Before summer Harcourt, Brace had lost the future work of Thomas Merton, T. S. Eliot, Flannery O'Connor, Robert Lowell, John Berryman, Jean Stafford, Bernard Malamud, and others. Not all these authors would follow Giroux directly, but all would end up on his list, some after a stop at a way station. In losing him, Harcourt had lost its most dedicated literary editor. Denver

Lindley, out of a sense of duty, stayed on to keep the Harcourt list from further erosion, but after a year or two he also succumbed to the strain imposed by the new management and departed for the Viking Press.

My own reaction to the palace revolution combined panic with distaste. As the weeks went by after the first resignations, half of every day's working time was given over to conspiracy, to gossip and speculations about Jovanovich's next move, to what the stockholders might do next, to whether a particular executive would make his peace, to whether such and such an author might leave. In public we were all expected to pretend that nothing was going on that was not perfectly normal, while in the office we kept looking over our shoulders to see whose door was shut.

In my innocence I could not have imagined that such struggles could so deeply affect my daily life. My confidence in the craft of editing dwindled, my belief in the constituency of authors and readers was cracked, and I awoke from my illusion of being one of the curators of a great list to realize that I was only another worker in another business. I sat in my cubicle reading the page proofs of Richard Wilbur's translation of *The Misanthrope:*

> And not this man alone, but all humanity
> Do what they do from interest and vanity;
> They prate of honor, truth, and righteousness,
> But lie, betray, and swindle nonetheless.
> Come then: man's villainy is too much to bear;
> Let's leave this jungle and this jackal's lair.
> Yes! Treacherous and savage race of men,
> You shall not look upon my face again.

My contempt and my instinct to flee were as facile as Alceste's. I had been willing to twist together the ill-suited strands of my life as long as I had an institution to believe in; but as that security crumbled, I finally resolved to get out of the city and start over.

My girl stood beside me devotedly as I came to the wary decision to change jobs, and my gratitude redoubled, so deeply that I even went so far as to ask her one night to marry me. The moment the words were out of my mouth I realized I had just made an impossible mistake. I felt as though I were turning to stone in her arms, as paralyzed by fear as that day she had seen me collapse in the boat crossing Long Island Sound. She was decent and intelligent enough to ignore my offer, and not long afterwards we agreed resignedly to part. I was shaken more deeply than I realized by my incapacity to respond to her love.

I kept waiting for something to happen, and luck was with me. Eugene Reynal had first been a promotional whiz kid at Harper & Brothers, then founded his own firm, Reynal & Hitchcock, publishing with distinction through most of the 1940s. After Curtice Hitchcock's death he sold out to Harcourt, Brace, joining the larger firm as the director of its general publishing division. Eugene was a man who had never recovered from the riches and razzle-dazzle of his youth, and middle age did not sit well on him. Once Jovanovich forced Eugene's resignation from Harcourt, Brace, the rest of his publishing career seemed motivated mostly by the wish to cut a figure. His second firm, which he now proceeded to found, would publish books imported from Europe. With as much vindictiveness towards Harcourt, Brace as generosity toward me, Eugene steered me to a possible job with Harvard University Press, to which he was an adviser. It was a relief to think of returning to Cambridge and Boston, where I frequently visited old friends. After the first interview I made up my mind to go if Harvard would have me.

The director of the Harvard University Press was Thomas J. Wilson, a tall, shaggy, graceful Southerner, who combined warmth and candor to an unusual degree. He had changed his course in middle life, leaving a textbook career with Henry Holt and Reynal & Hitchcock after his wartime Navy service in order to enter the newly invigorated field of the university presses. My interviews with him impressed me deeply. Tom was a man at home inside his skin, confident without arrogance or pretension. Stooped but formidably tall, bald but bushy-browed, an addicted smoker who relished martinis, he had the ability to give courteous attention to widely divergent points of view without losing the power to decide between them. He was emotional yet considerate: he could lose his temper in an air-clearing burst of rage, and then instantly apologize in such a way as to make all well again.

Here, I thought, was a man I could trust as I would not again be able to trust an institution, an individual whose publishing policies were consonant with his claims, a boss with whom one could work as an equal yet serve with pleasure as a subordinate. My instinct was right: Tom never disappointed me. I did not, and was not expected to, agree with all his policies. It would have been a pleasure to work for him longer than the year I did.

My move to Boston represented a new search for a "home" that I could call "my own," but that meant in fact a search for a new, more reliable sense of self. I knew something was wrong with the way I had been living, but I was far from being ready to admit or understand how deep my inner distraction went, or how little improvement this last change of scene could bring about. I was consciously aware, however, that I was not meant for New York; in fact, my separation from country life for so many years had transformed my memory of it to an overcharged nostalgia for my Colorado childhood.

When I loaded the last bag into my little Austin late on the night of my twenty-seventh birthday, I hoped I was wiping the slate clean. I traveled all night. As soon as I had left my possessions in the apartment I'd rented in Cambridge, I drove on to take the ferry for Martha's Vineyard, where I spent a couple of weeks swimming, singing, and running along the beaches. The dark shadow of the city seemed a long way behind me, as I pranced my new freedom along the shores of the sunny, undemanding island.

V

The Farther Shore

I may look fine at the moment, but like you
I have capered and somersaulted in the streets
While, balanced upon my shoulders, someone's face
Smiled at my friends and answered the telephone. . . .

P. D., "To a Mad Friend"

I know my man. Purdy's a hard-nosed man.
Another round for us. It's good to work
With such a man. "Purdy," I hear myself,
"It's good to work with you." I raise
My arm, feathery in the dim light, and extend
Until the end of it brushes his padded shoulder.
"Purdy, how are you? How you doodle do?"

P. D., "Lunch at the Coq d'Or"

1.

In 1955 Harvard University was enjoying a noonday of influence and prestige. New programs, special institutes and area studies were being launched; gifted young scholars were revolutionizing, or even inventing, fields like linguistics, microbiology, medicine, artificial intelligence; while in economics, politics, and the law, Harvard's stock was rising even faster than its endowment. The Press was expected to make the most of the university's possibilities as a center of scholarship, both by publishing Harvard authors and by submitting outside authors to Harvard scrutiny.

Cambridge was in its last palmy days as a university town. The influx of business and professional people (psychiatrists, management consultants, executives of the computer and aerospace industries) had not yet transformed it into a fashionable bedroom suburb, and the Harvard faculty still resided, as only its most senior members can now afford to, near Harvard Square. Tall elms and maples still shaded the old frame houses, small shops, mixed neighborhoods, and quiet streets, but there was enough visible evidence of crowding to make it evident that this Cambridge could not last long.

My office at the Harvard University Press was a far cry from the gray, artificially lit cubicle I had shared in New

York. Glassed in on three sides, a summer sleeping porch at the back of a converted mansion, it looked out over more than an acre of pleasant grounds that had been planted with trees and shrubs and gave cover to birds and squirrels. A door connected directly with Tom Wilson's office, the former master bedroom. As his personal assistant I acted as Tom's representative with most of the senior members of the faculty. He trusted me and always backed me up, and my authority with the professors was borrowed as much from Tom's personal stature as from the Press itself.

In my position I was approached every day with requests to help fulfill the publishing ambitions of Harvard professors and others. I began to understand the importance of power in the academic world, where it is even more hungrily contested than elsewhere (as Henry Adams pointed out long ago) because everyone has so little of it. I was made much of and had to resist the temptation to imagine that I had some special virtue. My sudden popularity, I fear, derived mostly from the Press's strategic importance at the height of the publish-or-perish period.

I was fairly well suited to the job. As the young assistant to an older man I could conduct myself by precocious imitation without ever having to risk self-definition or self-exposure. I had a bit more difficulty, as usual, with my peers in age: my young secretary, for example, shared her time between Tom and me, and obviously preferred Tom's paternal style to taking instructions from a contemporary. I felt uncomfortable when I had to ask her to type a letter.

My work at the Press (unlike any publishing job I have held before or since) did not require me to read manuscripts after hours. I hoped to spend my spare time, at last, on my own writing. I imagined too that the time had come for me to find a wife. I had taken a small apartment with its own private entrance on a Cambridge side street. For the first time I lived altogether alone. I furnished the place with odds and ends of my parents' cast-off furniture from New York, but there was one indispensable symbol of adulthood lacking, and so I marched off to Sears, Roebuck and ordered a double bed on the installment plan. I settled in and waited. Nothing much happened. My apparent freedom was darkened by loneliness. It was all very well to work during office hours for a man you admired like a father, but I wanted women's company—a mother, a sister, a lover.

Soon after settling into Cambridge I got in touch with an attractive blond girl named Sylvia Plath, whom I had met twice at Smith College the previous spring through Alfred Kazin. She had been writing poems and stories as well as a thesis on "the double" in Dostoevsky. She had gone for literary advice to Alfred, who told me she had undergone an abrupt nervous breakdown not too long before he came to know her. When I first sought Sylvia out at Smith I was directed to the shining sterile infirmary, where she was sitting alone, resting up after an exam. She was dressed in the saddle shoes, the kerchief, the simple skirt-and-sweater combination of the time, but, in her, conventional prettiness and intensity of concentration formed a curious, even a disturbing alliance. She seemed feverishly enthusiastic about literature and asked me hundreds of questions about publishing. On my last visit to Northampton I took her for a drive in the country and underwent a sort of traveling interrogation.

I telephoned Sylvia at her home in Wellesley, and she sounded excited. She had won a scholarship to Cambridge University. She wanted me to tell her all about study abroad. She had never been farther from New England than New

York and Albany. I asked her to have dinner with me a few days later. She arrived in a white dress, with a deep suntan and thick hair turned blonder by the sun. She asked more and more questions, she seemed strangely elevated, and she hardly waited to be asked to slip into my new bed. Thereafter, to my surprise, we began to see each other all the time. She brought me manuscripts of her poems and lent me recordings of Dylan Thomas to play on my old phonograph. She introduced me to friends around Cambridge and took me home to meet her mother. The intimacy was pressed, stilted. For once it was not I who was forcing the pace.

I would drive to Wellesley to fetch her, cook her dinner, and drive her back to Wellesley very late at night. Her quest for knowledge was voracious: I felt as though I were being cross-examined, drained, eaten; yet when she told me about her life, her previous love affairs, her successes at Smith, it was as though she were describing a stranger to herself, a highly trained circus horse. The verses she showed me were not yet poems, and few were ever published, but they were promising, the work of a real poet still in embryo. They lay open to varied and contradictory influences—Dostoevsky, Elizabeth Bishop, especially Dylan Thomas. She wrote of herself as a panther, as an acrobat, as anything but a young girl, leaping at the walls of reality in her eagerness to testify.

I was taken aback by her impersonal appetite for experience, as unquenchable as her appetite for information. What she said, what she alleged, the ways she loved, lacked credibility. She was too exigent for me. I could not seem to hold my own with her, though I was older and presumably more experienced. Her friends seemed as baffled by her, yet as fascinated, as I. My growing incredulity relented only when, one night toward the end of the summer, lying rigid, she told me, as though she were being fueled from within, the long terrible story of her breakdown and suicide attempt, the same story she would elaborate and embellish later on in *The Bell Jar.*

Her narrative at this stage, only two years after the original event, lacked the clumsy irony, the defenses, the semifictionalized characters, the nastiness of temper that mar the novel for me. What I heard was a simpler, less poised, and more touching story. As she came to the end, shock treatment in the hospital and her subsequent slow convalescence, she expressed her gratitude for the help she had had, she was glad to be well again; but the episode still seemed to be the only period of her life that she could invest with any real emotion in retrospect. I was deeply moved; yet I was alarmed too by so dedicated an attention to the approaches to death, so molten an obsession. Had the stakes never been high enough to enliven her before or since? She spoke as though the gamble with her own life was the only thing that had really counted, the only experience that had ever taught her who she was. After I drove her home the twelve miles to Wellesley and returned through darkness to the empty bed, I felt appalled, as though I had gained admittance to an unspeakable region; yet it was the only time that I had felt really able to connect with her as a human being.

After her confession, although we went away together for a weekend to Martha's Vineyard, she quickly grew cool and impatient. No doubt she sensed my awe; she may even have despised it. In letters from England she adopted the attitude that ours had only been a lighthearted flirtation. She made me feel used, as I later discovered others in her life had felt used. There seems to me no question that in the ordinary ways of response to other people, to the presence of other human beings, she was somehow defective at this stage of her life. The undeniable stature of the *Ariel* poems, whose terrible exaltation could not have been foretold from her earlier work or from her incapacity to absorb life, was attained through a cataclysmic reversal of her identity which was worlds away from the half-woman she had shown me.

To use experience is of course the way of artists, but I have encountered very few who grasped fellow humans quite so inhumanly as Sylvia did then. As Alfred Kazin wrote of her recently, "The world existed just to be written about." No doubt there are others who, like me, long after her death still remember her chilly touch, the fingers of the succubus. When she found herself rocketing into art seven years later, just before her suicide, she sent me some of her last poems for *The Atlantic* (we published several, but others have not yet seen print). I couldn't help being amazed that artistry of such stature could have emerged from so deficient a personality. But art, one comes to learn, can gain as much from pressure as from depth.

2.

I could not write. I would rather do anything than write. I was scraped with guilt and rage in Cambridge as in New York, but I plastered the scratches over and did everything and anything else—made music, played touch football, took ballet lessons, read Proust and Tolstoy. Finally, like many young people who have not yet learned the difference between acting their fantasies and living their lives, I gravitated to amateur theatricals. The Poets' Theatre had been founded in Cambridge several years before and had gathered around V. R. Lang, its guiding spirit, poets and actors like John Ashbery, Frank O'Hara, James Merrill, Mary Manning, Richard Wilbur, Edward Thommen, Tom Clancy and his younger brother Liam. In the autumn of 1955 the Theatre announced auditions for Molière's *The Misanthrope,* in the silvery translation by Richard Wilbur which I had read earlier in the year. The very thought of pronouncing those haughty couplets attracted me, and when I tried out for the play I was cast as Alceste.

We rehearsed for three or four weeks and then gave some twenty performances at the tiny Poets' Theatre near Harvard, and at the new Little Theatre at Massachusetts Institute of Technology. I had acted in school and college, but never before in one of the great parts of the literature. Alceste, the man whom everyone admires until enraged by him, who can find no one guiltless of hypocrisy, is at every moment two men, both a hero and a fool. Divided between nobility and petulance, he develops a scorn for mankind which amounts to a passion of thwarted idealism. His divisions, like Hamlet's, paralyze him and baffle his friends.

Every night for three weeks, I dressed in a long gray velvet coat, a brown peruke, and buckled shoes, and walked out into the glare of lights and the presence of an audience which laughed at Alceste's folly yet applauded his moral stature. I found these hours on the stage more real to me than my daily existence of tweeds, the office, groceries. Through Alceste I touched on myself.

Learning and reciting Wilbur's impeccable lines led me deeper and deeper into the behavior of the English language under the athletic discipline of strict rhymed verse. The freedom of the language within such arbitrary boundaries showed how far poetry could range, how much it could contain. It began to penetrate not only my mind but my body and my senses. For the first time I was participating in poetry from the inside.

Even after the run ended I remained aware of this new capacity. My father had come up from New York to see the play. When he went home he wrote me one of his infrequent letters.* It was as useful and benign as its tone was rare, and it must have cost him something to write it. He thought I had given a fine performance, sensitive yet strong, that I had mastered the language and the challenges of the part. It made him, he said, confident of his belief that I had a real talent for creative writing, and he urged me not to neglect it. I read the letter with growing excitement, for Alceste had already taught me that my father was right. His letter removed one of the imaginary obstacles, giving me as it were his permission to proceed, to speak (or sing) for myself. I was exalted at first, but fear followed almost at once. What would my writing reveal if I were to let it free? My unconscious knew all too well. My response, rather than striking out alone for the farther shore, was to panic, to thrash about, fleeing my father again to take refuge in the sheltering arms of women, clutching at a weak companion with whom I might sink to the bottom.

There had been a Radcliffe girl hanging around the Poets' Theatre, understudying and helping the stage manager. She was young, disturbed (she was undergoing psychoanalysis), childish, and succulent. Her own troubles thrust her at me, and I yearned toward her, for I sensed we were in the same boat. We went off and conspired together in bed like children, we argued and lamented. It all seemed so familiar.

* My father regarded letters, both writing and receiving them, with an almost ceremonial anxiety. As a young man, he had actually kept score in his diaries: had my mother written him as often as he had her? During the war years he invented a fictitious correspondent, his "former governess," Miss Letitia Blenkinsop, who indited epistles to my sister and me, to our unending delight, from far-flung outposts and in the most elevated Victorian English. After I visited England myself, his letters to me turned self-consciously paternal, as though something was called for. Still later, he would telephone me long distance to announce that he had just written me a letter, actually telling me everything it contained before he hung up.

At Christmas I attended a meeting of university presses at Princeton. During the sessions the faces and voices of my colleagues came to me out of a strange underwater distortion, paler and larger than life, hollow and sinister. I spent Christmas itself with my parents in New York and found the flayed intensity of my reactions hard to bear. I went one evening to a performance of O'Neill's *Long Day's Journey into Night* and emerged from the theatre feeling as though the flesh had been stripped from my bones by witnessing the tragic cycle of parents feeding on their children and children striking back to destroy their parents and each other.

When I returned to Cambridge I asked the Radcliffe girl about her psychiatric treatment and confessed that I was beginning to consider the same course. She was overwhelmed with gratitude. Only someone who has undergone psychotherapy knows how eagerly the patient wants everyone else to be a patient too. We clung to each other. That night she slept at my apartment in some act of imaginary sacrifice, but without telling me she was violating the dormitory rules. She was found missing from Radcliffe and was promptly expelled. I felt as guilty as if I had "got her in trouble." I no longer knew what to make of my emotions. I felt like an accident going somewhere to happen. Might I even become dangerous? I wanted help, and quickly.

3.

My Boston doctor, a sympathetic and gifted young physician named Robert Buka, helped me find a psychiatrist. (Buka died in a fire a year or two later, having rushed into the blazing ruins of his house to save one of his children—who had already been rescued.) The psychiatrist he referred me to, a Dr. G., was a skilled and subtle practitioner of Freudian psychotherapy with a particular interest in young patients. He had deep currents of courtesy and kindness in him, qualities not very usual in any profession. For three years, beginning in early 1956, I visited his office at least once a week. I expected psychotherapy to free me from the imagined grip of my family and to liberate my frustrated will to write. Even though I could by now label my problems clearly enough, it took a remarkably long time for me to assimilate my feelings.

The struggle between the doctor and myself (for so as a patient in the throes of transference I conceived it) seemed to take place in a clear dark pool at the center of my life. Little else during the next three years seemed as intense and innate as these hours, even though, as I began to awaken to myself, my ordinary life took on more vividness than it had known since I was a boy. As I began to learn how to love, how to release the poetry in myself, how to prevent new events from masking themselves with the remembered faces of the past, my existence crystallized in that small, dark, inconspicuously furnished doctor's office where I sat in a leather armchair carefully set so that if I wanted to see Dr. G. I would have to turn my head. The light fell on the side of his long face. He blandly smoked and listened, encouraging me both with his words, which were rare, and his silences, into which I read my own range of meanings.

The world of the patient in psychotherapy is made up of fantasy upon fantasy. No matter how well traveled its patterns have become, it can never be easy to face the fact that your fantasies are *you,* and to find yourself involved in the age-old oedipal tangle with your heart pounding and your tears hot on your face. As I sat in the patient's chair hour after endless hour, whatever I thought myself to be talking about came back sooner or later to Him, the presence barring the way, an antagonist keeping Her from coming through the door. No aggression of mine, no fury or scorn, could change my guilt and antipathy, not since the terrible time-stopping shock of my hand striking my father's face. My only way to circumvent Him and get to Her was illness, which would bring Her to my side—but at what a sacrifice! My rage must exclude my natural gentleness; my illnesses must obscure my natural strength.

To have adjudged myself "ill," to have accepted help and lowered myself into the chair opposite the doctor's desk, seemed in itself a confession of defeat. After my first hour of talk months went by in which I used every resource to fulminate at the very existence of my father. In dreams my father shifted his shape formidably, from a toothless policeman to an antlered elk, or took on guises of familiar living men as varied and bizarre as Robert Frost, C. G. Jung, John Kenneth Galbraith, Tom Wilson, and President Eisenhower. In other dreams I sought mysterious treasures in underground mazes, pleasures in murky pools. I balanced on high places afraid to jump and watched a puppy drown in the water below. I wandered by the side of Walden Pond and gazed in guilty horror at the naked bodies of boys and girls slithering together in the turbid water. The key dream, however, the dream of the City and the Island, came to me during the first weeks. I savored and handled it over and over until I knew it as well as myself, for it *was* myself.

I was floating far from land in a tiny coracle, a frail thing of sticks and hides that bobbed on the waves of the sea. My sister, a little baby, huddled in the same boat with me, like a fellow nestling. She was menstruating, an infant bleeding as though she were a grown woman. The waves swelled high enough to capsize us, but somehow they did not. We rose to each crest and coasted down the other side. Off to the right, on what should have been the California shore, lay a great smoking city, Philadelphia, the place of brotherly love, of adulthood, complexity, and skill. I paddled with my hands to make the coracle move toward the City, but the craft was held in the grip of a strong current which drew it out to sea, farther away from the City, towards Easter Island, remote country of archaic presences, of solitude, of childhood.

Try as I might, I could not make headway toward the shore and bring my sister back to Philadelphia, to get her out of the coracle/nest to the place that would cure her bleeding. (Or was the bleeding mine?) The ocean current tugged our frail boat towards the lonely heights of Easter Island, those close-cropped pastures, those massive stone-chinned masks. Yet I suddenly found myself ashore in the City after all, wandering alone through a smoggy darkness down winding streets out of whose upper windows girls leaned, bare-breasted, beckoning to me with curving arms and smiling as I fearfully hurried past them. The streets never ended, the cobblestones never dried, the darkness never lightened. *This* was the place I had chosen for refuge!

The Presence that prevented me from attaining my wishes, from being cured and receiving love, was my father, who held the key to poetry and who governed the tides of anger that pulled my coracle away from the City. If I were to lie bleeding like a girl, my mother would rally to my side, yet she herself was not above hurting me, as she had done in the car accident, nor above taunting me, as she had done in an earlier dream. So long as I lay still and ill, looking to my father and not myself for strength, to my mother and not myself for health, I would never cease to be a child, bleeding in a wallowing boat. My refusal to face the specters produced dozens of secondary dreams, where I appeared in all sorts of flattering yet flawed disguises—the speedy sprinter who could run fast but not far; a loutish adolescent terrible with a club; a sweet castrated singer; the boy wonder of publishing who knew all the answers but stammered at meetings.

When I first entered Dr. G.'s office I knew two kinds of helplessness: I was drawn to almost any girl who desired me, and I could not bring myself to write. I could remember most of the events of childhood but none of its emotions. When they returned to my mind, as during psychotherapy they did in convulsions of renewed experience, they came with terrifying force. I wept with gratitude and pain as the old wounds opened. Gratitude came out of the knowledge, even with the pain, that I had a self after all. When I dreamed of myself as a child, I substituted my sister, my baby ally and adversary, the only other creature whom I had been able to love as I loved myself, hurt as I hurt myself. It was she, my ally against adult oppression, my sharer of play and pain, whose flesh I knew from bed and bath and table, whose breathing I heard at night and whose sobs and whispers I had shared. When my parents did not want me to come between them, they sent me to play with my sister. I had recast her as both playmate and adversary in my later affairs with women.

Life during this period was not all introspection, and some of it was perfectly mindless. I rose early on the mornings when I met Dr. G., who considerately scheduled my appointments at seven-forty so that I could take the subway straight from his office to mine. I put in a full workday every day and led a fairly busy social life. I did not even feel much of an economic pinch, for I lived simply, and the thirty dollars I paid the doctor each week out of my $6,500 salary seemed so well spent that it never even became an issue in the treatment.

4.

At about this time I received an offer from my old college friend Seymour Lawrence, the new director of the Atlantic Monthly Press, to join his editorial staff. It was a tempting offer, for *The Atlantic* had been publishing books of distinction for thirty-five years, and it was now going through a period of rejuvenation. Much as I admired and loved Tom Wilson personally, I found many of the clumsily written academic books published by the Harvard University Press both boring and extraneous. Some of the expedients through which books were recommended to the Press for publication could be called at best clannish and at worst venal. Might not the nexus of commercial publishing prove to be a more honorable and even a more objective way of evaluating a book? Besides, I missed the editorial fun.

Though Lawrence's overture tempted me greatly, I was not ready to say yes. I had only just begun at Harvard, and my private problems seemed overwhelming. When the offer was repeated six months later I had begun to work towards a solution: I felt ready. I went to *The Atlantic,* with Tom Wilson's blessing, in the autumn of 1956, and I have never had reason to regret the decision.

The new job had little effect at first on my personal life— less, at any rate, than my psychiatric treatment. Not very long after I had begun visiting Dr. G., I met at the Poets' Theatre a beautiful new girl who, like me, had recently turned to psychotherapy. Large but graceful, even statuesque, with wonderful blue eyes under a Phidian brow, and honey-blond hair, she carried herself with an unruffled placidity that misled most people, but the disturbed have ways of signaling to each other. She and I were quickly and powerfully drawn together, almost as strongly by anxiety as by love. For almost two years we saw each other every day.

Love with this girl was different from any before or since, the sort of love that can neither be lived with nor lived without. I was partly adult and partly a child, and so was she. We shared physical love and exchanged mental fantasies. Our loyalties were split by our psychiatric transferences. We could not tell how much of our emotional attraction we owed to natural causes, and how much to those hours of dreaming and free association and self-absorption which we spent under the eyes of our doctors. We both knew that part of our hunger for each other was suspect, but not what part.

In my fantasy life my girl often took the role of my sister, both as my ally against parents and society and as my companion in the angry flight in the coracle. Her family had a marvelous place on the sea at Manchester, northeast of Boston, with several houses scattered through the woods looking down across sharp pink-and-orange sandstone cliffs towards offshore islands haunted by the sound of waves and the cries of gulls. We watched the blue changeable sea and the guano-whitened offshore rocks and reefs which seemed magically to float in the sea passage from Portsmouth to Boston. We felt ready to defy the adults in the houses along shore and push off in quest of the islands. My girl had been haunted for years by her family home, and now I focused on its acres and seashore all of my own suppressed hunger for the country: I was perhaps as much in love with Calypso's island as with the nymph herself. We talked endlessly about our families, we stole away on trips like children running away from home, we slept in and out of one another's apartments but never actually lived together. We talked of permanence as though it were a sea-girt dream and clung to our nightmares as though they would never end.

In time, however, we realized that we could never love each other enough. Too much of our love was based on precisely what we wanted to free ourselves from—neurosis, anxiety, self-hatred. In the end it was she who found the strength to give up the affair, and her strength only served to intensify my own sense of being weak. Yet the moment she left me, I could no longer pretend, as I had till now, that my love of women was heartless, pleasureless, painless, or indifferent. I devoted myself, like a troubadour, to taking pleasure in despair. Psychotherapy has a way of encouraging self-dramatization, and now I was involved in the self-consciousness of writing poetry as well. I scourged my normal grief and pain until I bled; once started I found it hard to stop.

I could not sleep, and I did not try to. I paced the streets in the snow of that winter, skulking near her apartment in the hope, and the fear, of seeing her; and finally, late on one of the coldest nights, I saw, with a gasp of pain as the spear went in, what my self-destructive angel had been seeking for me: in a car, on the street, in the other man's arms, she was embraced and embracing. I cried out loud and ran away trying to erase the picture from my mind, but it was seared into the brain itself: she was kissing *him*, kissing him hard; the car windows were steamed over. Her arm around his neck was embracing him more passionately than she had ever embraced me.

For weeks I labored to keep this pain alive. I found new girls, chased and laid them with dogged initiative, trying to wipe out—or stamp in—that memory. The girls who were attracted to me then were still little less unstable than I was myself, but there was a new callousness in me now, a selfishness. I watched myself moving toward a new candidate with distaste, even horror, reaching for her as a drunkard reaches for a bottle. To stop it, I worked at my office, hours every day and hours after the workday was over, Saturdays and Sundays, reading, editing, scouring magazines for new writers, writing articles of my own, and doing very little good.

For two or three months, in fact, I was crazier than I had ever been, driven to reenact every impulse that psychiatry had shown me to be foolish and self-destructive, every infantile compulsion that I could dredge up, wallowing in my self-disgust like an animal in carrion. I was punishing myself for being weak enough to lose, though what I had lost was, I knew, not really what I had wanted. My behavior was sufficiently serious to frighten me and alarm my friends, at least until they got bored with the performance. Though my pain arose from a half-trumped-up case, it was real, the danger was present. Unquestionably I looked over the edge and with an accident of timing or ill fortune I could easily have slipped, or jumped over. Perhaps what preserved me was my newly discovered capacity to write; it served me as a safety valve. I wrote now because I had to, because writing had become integral to my life. This had been the fourth deep depression of my life, the most protracted and the most painful, but it was also the first one from which, hand over hand, I finally managed to extricate myself by my own efforts, and without running away.

5.

Poetry came to me first in a trickle, then in a rush. I can almost name the hour it began. On an evening in August 1957, when I was twenty-nine, I was reading the manuscript of the *Selected Poems* of Stanley Kunitz, which was to be published by the Atlantic Monthly Press. The austere cadences of Kunitz's work began to generate a strange mood in me. I stood up and walked unsteadily to my desk. The poem I wrote had, I thought, to do with a friend of mine, the novelist Edwin O'Connor, whose incapacity to express openly the warmth of his feelings made him and me uneasy, as two who could not confess their capacity to feel pain. But of course the poem was not about my friend.

THE WINNER

I hear a child inside,
Crying to be let out.
"No," shouts the swaggering Self,
"Mind shall destroy all doubt.
Out with all doubt, I say!
Stifle that treacherous word!
I have high deeds to do
Twirling my deathly sword."

Mind's on his mettle now,
Deft at his surgical art,
Stunning my pain with pain,
Drowning the infant heart.

From now on I wrote all the time, trying to teach myself the craft of poetry in sonnets, stanzaic exercises, rhymes, and meters. My postponed adolescence surfaced in the bitter laments I wrote for the end of my great love affair, but none of these poems had any value except as sentimental discharge, and after a while I threw them away. They took on my father's accents, the accusatory voice of a man betrayed by women, the rhymes and reasons of a prewar world. In order to discover a voice of my own I had to get past this barrier. I filled up and discarded whole notebooks; reams of paper disappeared into the maw of trial and error, into dozens of stammering, uncertain revisions. The poems survived or dissolved of their own accord. For each one that I found worth keeping, I must have torn up half a dozen. Now and then I would find myself realizing that this or that poem was not bad enough to discard but could not be revised any further. It would have to stand.

At first it was hard for me to draw a line between the shadowy regions of psychoanalysis and the even more obscure spaces out of which poetry might emerge. Dr. G. discriminatingly helped set the boundaries. Fantasies useful for clinical purposes did not necessarily furnish material for poetry, nor did my poems often give me psychiatric understanding.

I began to write poetry reviews for *The Atlantic*. How many ways there were of saying a thing! How intimately a poet's style grew out of his poetic identity! I began to read and study not only younger poets trying, like me, to launch a style, but poets in their prime who had succeeded in changing their identity, driven by the need to grow: Theodore Roethke, John Berryman, Robert Lowell, John Hall Wheelock; and others, like my father, who did not or could not change.

During 1958, externally the stormiest year of my life, I began gradually to hear my own voice as a poet. The wound caused by my girl's leaving me began to heal over in spite of my efforts to keep it open. I began to be able to accept my parents as human beings instead of as archaic Presences. I started to discuss with Dr. G. the possibility of terminating treatment.

With the growth of confidence that I could distinguish between my poetic imagination and my fantasy life, I began to write poems that dealt directly with personal experience, to put myself in. The surface of poetry has little resemblance to the surface of life: even personal, "confessional" poetry has little to gain from realism. As I began to test the impersonality of the poet's art, I began to measure the distance between the poet and his life. It is only in the depths that the two touch one another. I began to realize that the writing of poetry was as necessary to me as work, sex, and competition. Writing was not something to be performed as precocity or bravura. Poetry was my way of keeping alive. No matter how precariously I might be floating in the cockleshell of my life, I now had something better than my hands to scull with, something I had fashioned and knew how to use.

Once I knew this, I turned back to the unconscious population of my dreams to see how the various spectral presences would react. Since my girl had left me I had been afraid to move too far from either the psychiatrist's office or my own. But my journeys of the past in the mountains, across Italy and England, through Kansas and across Long Island Sound, had all brought me revelation. Now, during my doctor's vacation, I resolved to try a real journey from the city to islands, to reenact the dream of the coracle to see if I could learn to master its terrors.

I flew to San Juan with dozens of families dressed in their Sunday clothes for the midnight flight from the *barrios* of Spanish Harlem to visit their Puerto Rican kinfolk. After a few days in Saint Thomas I found a berth on the deck of a rough-timbered schooner as she made her way eastward towards the open ocean. The black deckhands and passengers asked me if I was a Jehovah's Witness "by any chahnce?" "No." "Then you will not mind having a little drink with us from time to time? Manhattan wheesky, feefty years old," they assured me, bringing out a huge wicker-covered bottle of raw black rum. By the time we were east of Saint John's I was violently seasick.

I woke to see the volcanic pinnacle of Saba, for all the

world like Easter Island, rising on the horizon, with the pearly clouds of a tropical dawn swathing it like a garment. We landed at Saint Martin, and the schooner went no further, so I stayed a week. I went to a native Saturday-night dance in the hills where the drums beat like hearts and young couples slipped away into the darkness. Here my time ran out. I returned to San Juan and flew home.

The journey, despite the excitement and adventure of going, had proved strangely difficult, as though my limbs were heavy or the air were light. The smooth sea, the mountains sprouting greenery, the slow beautiful blacks in the streets and shops, all entered my consciousness as unreal. I watched and peered but could not bring myself to speak. Putting the city at my back, I had set off in a small boat in search of islands. Is it strange that something so simple to describe should prove so difficult to perform? No stranger than that a young healthy male should find it hard to obey his emotions, to exercise his gifts, or to fall in love.

My sister met my plane at the airport in New York. My mother had been taken to the hospital with severe pains in her back. Cancer was suspected, and an immediate operation was called for. My father would not permit surgery until he knew what I thought about it. My sister and I drove into New York together in a fearful silence.

So this was what lay at the end of the journey. My thirty-year childhood was coming to an end at last. Perhaps it ended when I stepped off the plane. Those presences that I had pursued among the islands were based on real, mortal people. Symbols were only symbols. "The world," says Santayana, "is not a myth, to be clarified by literary criticism." It had not really occurred to me before that my mother could die. Could it be that my life was less imaginary than I had thought?

VI

In the Clearing

When I was a child, a heartstruck neighbor died
On her birthday. Dying was strange enough,
But what a way to choose to spend your birthday,
I thought, and what sort of a gift was this?
From time to time, people have done it since—
Dying in the environs of a celebration
As though they had picked out the day themselves.
Perhaps they had, one way or another,
Prayed for something to happen, and prayed wrong.
Sophocles, when old enough to die,
Suspected prayer and entered a caveat:
"Zeus, act kindly whether or not I pray;
And, though I plead for it, turn harm away."
I keep a wary silence on my birthdays,
Make up no lists at Christmas, lie low
When asked what I *really* want. How should I know?
Best ask for gifts as though I had none coming.

P. D., "Gifts"

1.

Once I began to write poems I could no longer deny that I had come into a direct inheritance from my father and had to do something with it. It scared me. Even with his blessing and encouragement I felt caught by the ankles in those old patterns of evasion that had governed me since childhood, hiding strength under weakness, hiding weakness under strength. How was I to put myself, my true self, forward? I had never felt free to speak out in company (my parents smiling uneasily in case I made a mistake) unless I could be sure that what I said would please them. Any utterance of mine, including the written word, might violate the warning so often evoked in a household of talkers—"Don't interrupt!" I had to learn to speak my own words without stepping back into that parlor of approval.

The burden of the past was not cast off during those troubled months of 1958—it never is—but it was shifted so I could walk. My father had endowed me with a certain power. It was a gift, a gift with the magic properties of that word, a poisoned apple. The awe with which my father gave voice to the poems he recited had imbued me with the same veneration for the magic properties of poetry. Now I had to face inheriting some of the same powers of the shaman. A mystery—as mysterious as the relation of the soul to the body.

> How with this rage shall beauty hold a plea
> Whose action is no stronger than a flower?

My father's talent, misused and betrayed though it had often been, was the principal gift he had left. I had struggled for years to discriminate between the bearer and the gift without success. Only in those tatters of rebellion that I flew during the years of adolescence did I allow myself to disapprove, silently, of the mistakes he had made in the cultivation of his muse and lament how his gift had been wounded by discontent. On one side my love for the man, tainted by the instinctive antagonism of Oedipus for Laius. On the other, awe for his gift, mingled with scorn for the way in which the shaman had betrayed his calling. I resolved, as young men will do, never to repeat my father's mistakes, not knowing yet what peril lies in such resolutions.

I resolved not to repeat my father's mistake in the choice of a woman. I thought my mother had been better suited to be the mother of a poet than the wife of one: the contention between my parents could not ever be fully healed by singing, any more than it had been between Dylan and Caitlin Thomas.

I resolved not to swallow my father's faith that a poet could rely on "being a poet." Poetry is a gift, not a role. We like our poets to dress themselves as sages or clowns or antiheroes: only then, it seems, do we allow them to play a part in society. Eliot the old possum; Dylan Thomas the drunken clown; Pound the village explainer and scapegoat; Ginsberg the hero of the counterculture; Stevens the cagey businessman and elitist. Only Frost could be said to have earned his way as a performing poet, but he paid a price, and though Eliot

earned a publisher's salary, he will probably be longer remembered in this capacity for declining twice to publish
George Orwell than for any other reason. Would there ever
be a way of playing the role without corrupting the self or
the poetry? To allow oneself to be patronized by an institution, whether a university or a foundation, was healthy for
neither man nor institution. How many writers—Shakespeare
and Chekhov excepted—had given the best of themselves all
their lives long?

Though I had been retarded in coming into my poetic
inheritance, I had been lucky in other ways. When I began to
write seriously, at thirty, I was already trained as an editor
and had a base on which to earn a living. Book publishing
might be regarded as a "mere" way of supporting myself, but
I found it fascinating and absorbing in its own right. Publishing was an acquired characteristic, while poetry was genetic.
If I had not come upon it relatively late, I might have come
to regard poetry as the perennial avocation of an amateur,
but when at last I discovered my gift, I learned I could take
poetry lightly only at the risk of severe damage to myself.
Though the worldliness of publishing, with its mission of
serving writers, gave me pleasure and a sense of involvement,
my poetry, emerging at times from its underland, was vital to
my wholeness.

There is no point in pretending that I arrived at this
understanding all at once without a thousand false moves
first. Regardless of how my father or others responded to my
work, I had to depend on myself alone to recognize the true
signs of that mysterious gift of which I had been given inter-
mittent custody. Many of the signposts lay in my childhood.
While I continued to develop the skills of an adult, I must
recognize that poetry's alertness was that of the child.

Eliot had said once, truly, that ninety percent of an editor's time is devoted to projects which come to nothing. Since publishing is not only a collective but an intermediary activity, this can't be helped. Editors are continually frustrated in communicating their enthusiasm for a book to the public; it is always easier to publish the authors you don't want than the authors you do. The authors you admire normally disagree with you on where their interests lie. Any publishing office, like any other office, offers the opportunity for differences and quarrels with colleagues and rivals. Abrasions like these sometimes made a life in poetry seem like a desirable escape—but I had watched my father's face over half a lifetime and knew that poetry was no way to escape from the most terrible confrontations with the self. Far better the distractions of publishing, the welcome ring of the telephone, the calculations of profit and loss, the estimates and negotiations, the concerns with authors' troubles, the sense of being able to help, to serve a need and plead a cause. It would always be easier to live with such entanglements than to stare helplessly at an unfinished poem in which you knew you had not dared, or had failed, to tell the truth. There is no concealing your shortcomings from the unfinished poem, though success, on the rare occasions you attain it, is unmistakable. It's no accident that poets have always described their art as the most demanding, and the most desirable, of mistresses.

My entry into poetry was not vouchsafed to me until I had reached and touched the first talismans of my life as a grown man. My first total love affair, a failed one. My passage out of the apprentice stage in publishing and arrival, at the Atlantic Monthly Press, at a position where I could trust, and execute, my own adult judgments. My coming to terms, assisted by Dr. G., with my father's existence as both a donor and a competitor. But the most important event of all was my first whole and reciprocated love, the love of my wife.

Both marriage and the acceptance of my gift came to me in my thirtieth year, which was the same year that I learned that my mother was going to die. It would be easy to speak off-handedly about the substitution of one dependence for another, but there could be nothing glib in so fatal a knowledge. I could not accept independence until I recognized its authenticity beyond the vaporous posturings of an adolescent. I could neither publish books in my own way, nor love in my own way, nor write poetry in my own way without accepting the gifts I had inherited as well as those I had acquired. The gift, the poisoned apple, gleamed with the knowledge of death and madness. Only by accepting it could I accept the embrace of life.

I met my wife, Jane Truslow, in the fall of 1958, not long after my return from the Caribbean. It was a lucky moment for both of us, and we opened to one another without hesitation. My mother's illness and a dozen other unsettled questions cast a shadow, but within a few days of our first meeting Jane and I knew that all we had to agree between us was not whether we should marry, but when. It turned out to be the easiest as well as the crucial decision in my life.

2.

Mount Sinai Hospital in New York is not unlike other American hospitals, those elementary schools where most of us learn about mortality. Hospitals and schools even resemble each other architecturally: the older buildings have high ceilings and gloomy interiors; the modern rooms are low, crowded, and sleazy. We found my mother lying uncomfortably in bed under a high ceiling, looking drawn and worried. She had never had much tolerance for pain. She was undergoing a series of diagnostic tests. Nothing could be decided until the laboratories produced their results. The doctors had little to say yet. After talking to them and my father, I went back to Boston, promising to return when needed.

The diagnosis turned out to be a cancer indeed. It had begun in a kidney and spread through the body via the bloodstream, touching both lungs and possibly lodging in the backbone as well. The doctors recommended: first, removing the affected kidney by surgery; second, treating the lung and backbone by chemotherapy (in this case, mustard gas) and hoping for a remission of the cancer's spread. The operation was performed, and she responded well to it. Things took a short turn for the better.

We did not openly or often discuss what was wrong. My mother knew her plight as well as we did, but she had always cultivated euphemism in medical matters. Even before her illness she hated to utter "cancer," and we did not disoblige her by insisting on the word; but this lowered a veil between us. My future conversations with her, unlike the confessions of the past, would be affected, sometimes seriously, by this inhibition of candor. Because of my father's equally primitive dread of the disease, the doctors seemed to prefer to talk to me rather than to him when decisions were required, and I was repeatedly telephoned in Boston or summoned back to New York to advise whether to operate, to hire a nurse, to move my mother to a different hospital, to ask for further consultations. I traveled to New York almost every weekend in order to discuss progress with the doctors, to cheer up my mother, to keep my father from pitying himself too much or drinking too hard, and to console my sister, whose emotions in this emergency were bound to be close to my own. But I was also courting my wife, and my new authority, the adult stature that both situations thrust on me, were bewildering, unexpected, and a little heady. I got angrier and angrier at my father as the weeks and months went by and he made no effort to recover charge of the situation, to take back his responsibilities. Of course this produced guilt as well. How can any child accept, with a clear conscience and a joyful heart, the adult powers which come to him through the debilitation and destruction of his elders? If I was faced with accepting the gifts of maturity, love, and poetry all at the same time, it was not entirely a matter of choice.

My mother recovered well enough from her operation to enable my parents to depart for Europe in March 1959, when my father was due for a sabbatical leave from Hunter College. Jane and I decided to be married before they left. There was a small Episcopal wedding in New York, after which we drove off to Peacham, Vermont. Our friends, the Howard Mumford Joneses, had lent us their farmhouse there as a wedding present. It snowed and snowed and snowed. When we could shovel ourselves out, we skied, and then it snowed some more. My parents took an airliner to Spain.

After the honeymoon Jane and I returned to Cambridge to set ourselves up in my treetop bachelor apartment. Soon afterward I had to go south on a business trip, several times postponed owing to the personal stresses of the previous year. I had not been gone more than a few days before Jane telephoned me in Atlanta with word that my mother had suffered a relapse in Spain and was returning home. When I got to New York, my mother was moaning in a bed in the Memorial Hospital for Cancer and Allied Diseases, where she was being prepared for another operation, this time a spinal fusion. It would not stop the cancer, only perhaps reduce the pain.

The summer and early fall of the year saw her decline every week. Jane and I shuttled back and forth the two hundred miles to New York on the weekends, but we couldn't do much good. The polarization between my parents was gradually being dissolved by the caustic of illness. My father did not ride out the emergency well. At bad times he seemed almost to imagine that it was by my mother's will that this disease had seized her, so as to cause *him* distress. Though he anesthetized himself with whiskey, there was no analgesic for my mother's indignity and suffering. She was deprived, one by one, of all her qualities—first her vitality, then her equanimity, then, gradually, her speech. She was not even blessed in her long decline with a loss of reason. She knew what was happening to her, but she could not make herself understood. The cancer had eaten its way into her brain, and the speech centers were affected first. Her words became garbled, edgeless, unintelligible.

One day in the late summer, as I sat alone beside her hospital bed, she pulled herself together and, staring at me wildly, her face writhing with the effort, managed to pronounce, so that I could have no doubt of what was being said, "I . . . think . . . I'm . . . dying." Was it a question? I had no answer: I could not say no, nor could I bear to say yes. She was asking me for help in her death. Whatever strengths I had gained, they were not enough. I squeezed her hand and said nothing, pretending not to have understood what she was asking me. Then she went on, tired by her earlier effort, to ask another question, which I really did not understand.

I was sure that day that I knew what she wanted; now I am not so certain. I thought she was asking for relief, for a way out; but could she have been asking me merely to share the extremity of her plight, to hold her hand and speak to her truthfully? That did not quite occur to me: I believed it was up to me to *do* something. I spoke to her doctors and told them she knew the truth, but when I asked them if there was anything they could do to soothe her pain and let her go peacefully, they looked at the floor. Miracles had been known to happen, there was no way except to keep trying, at least something could be learned from "her case" which would help other victims in the future. There was no way of knowing whether the doctors had heard my question, but I could not insist further. I returned to my mother's bedside to squeeze her hand when she tried to speak, to tell her of my new happiness with Jane, to assure her that all was well with me. What else could I say except to promise her that some kind of life would go on? But the doctors *had* heard me: when she died, the cause of death was pneumonia.

My mother's final months exacted so much that we couldn't look beyond the fact of her dying. It was not until years afterwards that I could reflect on the transformations of her life. On her marriage to my father, she became his enthusiastic companion in a literary life. While he was riding the lecture circuit during their early years together, her letters to him speak only of her family or about "interesting people" in and around New York. Later, in our Colorado years, she eagerly welcomed the birds of passage—writers, musicians, and others—who stopped off in Boulder on their way from coast to coast. In those years she was guilty of believing that writers and artists were the only people worth knowing.

In Washington during the war, in her forties, she found herself in a very different world, among publicists, activists, journalists, soldiers, administrators, politicians. Her job in the Office of War Information, administering programs and serving on committees, gave her a professional identity which did not depend in any way on my father's. Thenceforward she spent more and more of her time in politics.

Although she kept her devotion to kinfolk and to her old friends, her calm and her beauty began to be spent in rigging herself out for the guerrilla campaigns of reform politics, the meetings and endless telephonings about who and when, the obligatory political alliances in which camaraderie masqueraded as friendship. In her youth she had been both cruel and generous, stubborn and combative, romantic and an intellectual snob, energetic and intuitive. Middle age took hold of her and she found herself gnawing bones of disappointment, as she watched her husband's talents atrophy and his artistic energy flag. She must have felt a practical as well as a personal necessity to cultivate an identity beyond that of his wife. But in transforming herself she mislaid a part of her resources and stifled the self which had fired her youthful bohemianism —yet who is to say whether she had any choice?

As she watched my father sag away from the self-confidence of the practicing artist, stiffen out of poetry, shrug away from teaching, and become gradually mesmerized by drink and nostalgia for Cambridge and London, her loyalty would not permit literal unfaithfulness. Yet she must save herself: she could not go down with my father, no matter how tight his grip. So she acted the part of his wife with good grace and diverted her deepest feelings into passionate parenthood. She clucked over my sister, trying to protect her from all the blows life might prepare. She gossiped on the telephone with her amazing mother every day, and visited her often.

Although she did her best to keep up the appearances of marriage (though in fact she probably never thought of them as "appearances"), her eyes had turned away from her husband. My father, with unerring scent, knew her aversion for what it was. He knew that her pride would not let her lie to him, but that the same pride would never permit her to separate their outer lives. He knew that she felt she had used him up.

My mother was not the sort of woman to admit her decision to herself, and even less likely to admit it to anyone else. Only once did she unburden herself to me explicitly. Not, characteristically, in conversation (that would have been too embarrassing), but in a long letter which I received at Cambridge University when she was about fifty. It ended: "If something doesn't change, we're in for trouble." By the time I returned to New York, something *had* changed. She had. She had urged her life into a new direction, cultivating her will rather than her spirit. It might better have been done three decades earlier.

In the nine years that remained to her after her decision, my mother spun farther and farther away from her youthful intimacy and subtlety. The attrition of her marriage, the adulthood of her children, the public yearnings of her liberal spirit, the by now heavily female orientation of her nearest of kin (her mother had been widowed, her sister had been widowed twice, her daughter was unmarried, I had moved away) —all these combined with the transformations of the menopause to alter her. She grew stout. Her features thickened. Her opinions grew more tenacious, more partisan. She depended more and more on the outside world and less on herself for reassurance of her identity.

The decline of her marriage, I now realize, deprived her as bitterly as it did my father. When the cancer came on, few spiritual resources remained to withstand the corrosions of fear and physical agony. She had no safeguard like the poetry that my father was bound to like a wheel. As she lay dying, she had lost, or had been deprived of, the certainties that my more fortunate grandmother, dying a year or two later at eighty-nine, still retained to the end.

On the afternoon of September 22, 1959, the day before my mother's sixtieth birthday, the telephone rang at my office in Boston. It was my father, speaking stiltedly from notes in an extraordinary choice of words: "Natalie expired at twelve-forty this afternoon. The cause of death was pneumonia." I flew to New York, and Jane followed as fast as our Volkswagen would travel. Now there was nothing left to do for my mother, and we had to take care of my father, who was understandably less able to handle the necessities of the situation than ever. I had a funeral and a cremation to arrange, obituaries to write, grief to soothe, for my father was pathetically eager to turn over everything to me, as though I might hold him responsible were he to make some "wrong" decision. Luckily Jack Priestley was in New York, and, along with my father's old Army friend S. L. A. Marshall, he sat with my father and the whiskey while I dealt with undertakers.

The service would, appropriately but tryingly, be nondenominational. My father asked me to say a eulogy on his behalf. I could not trust myself to speak without tears. Even before my mother died I had a prophetic dream in which I was required to stand up before a crowd of curious mourners and could think of nothing to say. As I had written in a poem anticipating her death:

> I had ransacked my pockets twice—no memoranda—
> And my Oxford Book of Consolations had vanished.

Jack Priestley paid her tribute instead in a heartfelt and eloquent eulogy.

The tragedy of aging, waning, dying, went beyond understanding. My mother's emptiness at the end, the loss even of the pride that had sustained her last years, seemed an intolerable insult. Even when I wrote of her death in a group of poems I could think of nothing but *my* grief, *my* loss, even though it was she who had lost everything. It was just the moment when the rewards of life were falling to me. I could not help the timing, but no doubt this is why the rare quality of her life, her bravery, her pride, quickly evaporated from my memory and has only, many years later, begun to return. The prayer I wrote after her death was not answered.

> The world now has
> A gray look to it.
> There is much less strangeness
> Left in strangers.
> Mountains have shrunk,
> Trees loom with less shadow,
> Even the flavor of fear
> Tastes as diluted.
>
> Yet the bloom of your presence
> Is absurd as unicorns
> Or buttercups at Christmas.
> Just as your girlishness
> Glanced out daily
> From within thickened
> Middle-aged flesh,
> So does memory
> Find you hovering
> In a hundred places
> Or standing
> At the center of the music.
>
> I pray you, do not stray
> Farther from us.

3.

In certain ways the months of my mother's dying were as hard on my wife as on me. The new daughter-in-law, always the "outsider" who threatens the old mother-and-son relationship, never has an easy time of it at best. Jane's initiation had been grimmer than most. She had carried off her role gallantly but it was not done without cost. It was time now for us to go away to let things heal in a different climate, and we planned a trip to Greece and Rome, Paris and London.

Traveling with Jane made things new, especially since we learned just before our departure, in the spring of 1960, that our first child was expected in the fall. Still, presences and echoes put in their appearance now and then. As we stood together looking down into the valley at Delphi, it seemed altogether believable to imagine that the oracle was still in residence, offering enigmatic explanations for the facts of death and birth. The cliffs towered behind us. Eagles (or were they vultures?) soared overhead, and down below lay the ancient sweep of olive orchards and the glittering Gulf of Corinth. Out of a cave in the very heart of this mountain flowed water, the Pierian Spring, the fountain of the Muses. I began a poem which, though it would take me several years, undertook to explain to myself the riddle of my origins. I felt at Delphi that I was connected to the navel of the natural world, that I had reached the destination of all inner and outer voyages, that I must reaffirm some umbilical connection to the past before my mother's existence vanished from memory.

When we arrived home in May, much had changed: even Delphi could not arrest time. Our first child was due in six months. My father had decided to marry again: when Jane and I landed in New York he introduced us to Rose Landver, a former diva, a consultant to the Metropolitan Opera, and the director of the Hunter College Opera Workshop. She became his wife in July. Not many months later my grandmother died, still grieving her daughter's death and only partly consoled by knowing that our son, the first Davison grandchild, had been born. (When we told my infuriating father that the child's name would be Edward Angus Davison, he paused before asking, with the utmost gravity, "Did you name him for anyone in particular?") My mother's half of my grandparents' estate, bypassing my father, was divided between my sister and me. I bought a house in Cambridge, a "home of my own."

In these last two years I had finished psychotherapy, taken a wife, lost a mother, gained a stepmother, fathered a son, lost a grandmother, and taken my first steps as a poet. Moreover, my sister had married a kind and delightful man, the musician Forrest Perrin. A few years earlier any one of these events might have precipitated a crisis. Taken together, they dissolved the intense little family that had shaded my existence for thirty years. My wife's family, an amiable and closely knit group whom I loved already, had a cheerful and far less exigent notion of family ties; and, after all, I had become the center of my *own* family. I had now to learn how I would act as a father. With our own roof over our head and a baby (eventually two) under it, life slowed and smoothed, lost its anguish and unpredictability. After so many years of worrying about who I was, I could concentrate at last on what I was doing.

My poems came to me regularly and unpredictably, and I kept notebooks to enter new ideas, phrases, lines, and sketches which I could develop late at night or early in the morning before work, or on weekends and holidays. The stream of poetry absorbed my need to explore the unremembered stretches of my childhood and the anomalies of my present existence. I gradually sharpened a technique and accumulated a body of work, and I gradually found I could face other concerns in my poetry than the mere question of its existence. The child in me was no longer confined to the inside: he had come out, was able to see and speak. I found broader stretches of territory available to my poetry, but my poetic memory ran in a different current from the ordinary stream of time, and I would often be surprised, as I still am, by finding in my notebook poems I did not remember having written.

I spent long days at my office and nights and weekends reading manuscripts at home, in addition to my office time, which was spent in decision-making, in managing the endless details of turning manuscripts into Atlantic Monthly Press books. I learned to organize my time, sometimes brutally, to resist the varied demands on it. I had to travel often, mostly to New York and elsewhere in the United States and Canada, to search for new authors and to try to learn what interested the reading public; and I sometimes interspersed these trips with public reading of my poetry at schools and colleges and writers' conferences.

4.

I had always found it easiest and most comfortable to learn from young women or older men, especially the old men. I dreamed that wisdom had floated to me on clouds of pipe smoke while I sat at my father's side, or at his feet. Now I needed more challenging teachers than my father. The most remarkable was Robert Frost, whom I remembered from childhood but whom I got to know on my own after my father took me to visit him my first week at Harvard in 1945.

Frost was one of my parents' greatest gifts to me. They had both known him for years. My mother was a friend of the eldest Frost daughter, Lesley, from Barnard College. My father had looked Frost up shortly after he came to America with a letter from J. C. Squire. They took to each other, and in 1927 Frost even suggested that Teddie write his biography. But, deviously, Frost thought better of it and pulled the boards out from under the project in such a way that my father never knew quite what had gone wrong. (The details of this curious episode are recounted in the late Lawrance Thompson's *Robert Frost: The Years of Triumph.*) After this, though meetings between the Davisons and Frost became less frequent, they did continue in Florida, Colorado, Washington, and elsewhere.

From the time I went to Harvard until his death eighteen years later, I saw more of Frost than my parents did. Sometimes he would come to dinner at my house, where I would invite a girl whom I wanted to impress, or a younger poet, or a mutual friend. More often I visited the old man in the late afternoon or evening at his Cambridge house on Brewster Street, where I would listen in the dark sitting room while he rambled on about Milton, or Jonas Salk, or American policy in China, or apple growing, or book publishing, or the United Nations, or his long, touchy relationship with Ezra Pound.

Listening to the old poet was like watching a conjuror lift a series of toys out of boxes and turn them glittering in the light. Each time he lifted up a toy, a new idea, a line from Milton or Emerson, to show it for a second time, it would have gained a glow from being handled. He tried on the sounds of words to see if they would fit his ideas, his jokes, his turns of wit. Often you could watch him working out a poem in conversation, testing an idea in different suits of clothes. I heard him, over many months of playing with the contrast between tools and weapons, finally come up with a couplet which had been solicited by the United Nations for their Meditation Room but which they of course refused:

> Nature within her inmost self divides
> To trouble men with having to take sides.

He tantalized his ideas as he juggled them, his voice scratching and rumbling as he sat almost motionless in his chair, slumped a little over his old man's big belly, his feet planted on the floor in thick, soft-soled shoes, his tie loosely knotted. Only his hands moved, up and down for emphasis with the motion of a woodcutter chopping, or rubbing wearily over his eyes as though brushing away cobwebs. His hands were burly and massive on their outer sides with the strength of a man who had done his own farming for a long time; but the palms looked as though they belonged to a different animal, milk-white, soft, as reticent as the knuckles were strong.

Though his talk was magical, I could hardly remember it after I finally had left him late at night, when we had walked together back and forth in the dark two or three times between his door and mine while he rambled on more flickeringly than ever, unwilling to quit while his mind was running well. My mother had written in 1929, during the summer my parents spent near the Frosts in Arlington, Vermont: "I wish his conversation weren't so very difficult to remember and reproduce. It is the best I have ever heard—yet I can scarcely remember more than two or three things I have ever heard him say. One reason is that it strings together very loosely, like an essay; starting with a doorknob and ending with a new conception of infinity."

One night in the late thirties in Colorado Springs Frost sat up very late with my mother alone and talked "very personally" to her. Those words were all she would ever reveal about the occasion, but I now think he confessed to her what he had done to my father. Fortunately my father died before

Thompson published the truth about the episode. My
mother had never told her secret while she lived.

Frost may have gone out of his way to be kind to me as
atonement for his old sin, or he may have taken a shine to me
on my own account. It was hard to tell, for he talked to
everyone the same way, without condescension and without
concession. His talk amounted to a style, and although everyone who knew him felt he knew him well, only a very few
members of his family and a handful of friends were ever
able to get behind the carefully modeled exterior.

> I have kept hidden in the instep arch
> Of an old cedar at the waterside
> A broken drinking goblet like the Grail
> Under a spell so the wrong ones can't find it,
> So can't get saved, as Saint Mark says they mustn't.

I am sure there were hundreds like me who felt that they
alone *really* understood his poetry, his way of talking and
thinking, his way of converting speech into thought and both
into poetry, for he had that rarest of qualities among writers:
his speech and his writing took the same voice.

I sat in his living room with the Andrew Wyeth watercolor
on one wall showing morning light leaking into an old barn.
I was happy listening to the wisdom of the old man, to the
gnarled cadences of his speech, hearing the poetry gleaming
out of it like precious metal. It was like those hours I had
spent in my childhood listening to my father on summer
evenings, but there was a difference. No fate bound this old
poet and me together, no undercurrent of rivalry, obedience,
or fear, only the unspoken acknowledgment that our fate—
mine too, whether I liked it or not—was somehow bound up
in poetry. In my years of repressing poetry, I had come closest
to freeing myself on those late spring and fall nights after I

left Robert at last on his doorstep and fell into my bed to ruminate on the movements of his speech, the ebullience of his words, the wittiness and singularity of his cadences. He lifted me up.

By the gleam of his attention Frost enabled me to believe that if I could hold his interest, there must be something in me that was worth uncovering. He went beyond that, once I had finally started writing poems in 1957, to ask me, every time he saw me, whether I had "anything to show him." I took to carrying a poem in my pocket to each of our meetings. Though he may have commented to others on what I wrote, he never said a word to me about any of my poems; but the next time he would inquire again, and I would leave another typescript or two.

In spite of his kindness to me, he had no insufficiency of mischief and malice. One evening at my apartment he saw on a table a copy of W. H. Auden's *The Shield of Achilles* and asked if he might borrow it. I wrote my name in the flyleaf and handed him the book. He asked to borrow my pen and began writing in the flyleaf himself. When I looked inside, the inscription read, the first two lines in his handwriting and the third in mine:

> To Robert Frost
> from
> Peter H. Davison

I never saw the book again until after his death, when I asked Kathleen Morrison, Frost's amanuensis of twenty-five years, if she could get it back for me, and she did.

At his house once, in 1948, he was describing a visit T. S. Eliot had paid him earlier that same day. Frost told how the two of them had discussed a fellow poet who, they agreed, was a generous borrower of other poets' styles and ideas. "Yes," said Eliot to Frost. "He borrowed from my translation of St.-John Perse's *Anabasis,* all the way through."

"I told him I hadn't read it," Frost reported to me. But the *Anabasis* was lying on the table in the hall outside the room we were sitting in where Eliot could not have failed to see it.

Robert was abashed when I told him so. "It is?" he stormed. "It is? I thought I had left it in the country. I thought I had left it in the country."

He had much to say about the art of poetry and about the oddities of a poet's life. He used to talk about meter as the strings of an instrument, immovable, across which the poet must strike the tune of his own rhythm. Once he said, "Some younger poets think the mind is dangerous and should be left out. Well, the mind is dangerous and should be left *in.*"

A piece of advice he kept giving young people, but which I never took, was to walk out, to drop out, to go it alone. He quoted Saint Paul: "Quit ye like men," he would snarl, with a terrible gleam in his eye. But he seemed keenly interested in and kept bringing up the duality of my commitment to publishing and to poetry, and he was pleased when I told him I found no insuperable difficulty in carrying on with my own work while earning a living publishing other people's books.

"Yeah," he said once in that croaking rumble of a voice. "Yeah. You can't write poems all the time, can yuh? Shifti-ness. It's a good word. Shifty. You gotta shift back and forth between loyalties. Loyalty to your work. Loyalty to your family. Loyalty to your country. Loyalty to God. You got to shift a little here and shift a little there to get along. But you gotta get along. Gotta shift. We say makeshift. Shifty. Nothing wrong with that. We gotta make shift."

I never told him about my private problems. He disapproved of psychoanalysis and would have been annoyed or contemptuous, perhaps, if he had known me to be engaged in the process—though possibly he guessed without my ever telling him. In the generous way he shared himself, however, he displayed a quality—kindness—that is seldom to be seen in his letters and which rarely if ever floats to the surface of Thompson's biography. It does not matter that with me he may have had his reasons, that he may have been in his furtive way repenting the injustice he had done my father years before, but kindness was the result, no matter what the motive. When I finished my first book of poems I asked Robert, even before its acceptance, if I might dedicate it to him and my father jointly, and he said yes, but he did not live to see it published. I wish he had, if only so that he could have taken a secret satisfaction in saying nothing about it.

Now, a decade after his death, and after the publication of the ambivalent volumes of Thompson's life, Frost's reputation has taken the customary zigzag. His public image (the old man fumbling, then recovering, his poetic balance at the inauguration of President Kennedy; his trip to Russia and his meeting with Khrushchev; the oaken, snowy-haired venerability that made him for a while as sanctified a figure as Longfellow or Tennyson, but as vulnerable to reaction as they) is no longer before us. Only the poetry, perhaps for the best.

That carefully nurtured public personality was one of his most ingenious inventions, as well as his most fallible. Partly because of it, his poetry was widely misread during his lifetime. I once heard him say, in connection with the poetry of his "rival" T. S. Eliot, "He doesn't want people to understand him. I want people to understand me, but I want them to understand me wrong." They did. By consciously and literally making himself plain-spoken—which I believe he achieved as a deliberate act of will in his late thirties ("I stole the goblet from the children's playhouse")—he developed an extraordinary voice of his own, but his speech and his poetry were so artful in their simplicity that most of his readers contented themselves with the sound of sense ("Weep for the little things that made them glad") and missed the subtlety of the art, the ambiguity of his imagery, the terrible contradictions which, at war beneath his mask, made him a great poet.

He was indeed a great poet—America's greatest, my father and I agreed in thinking, though we did not always agree on poets or poetry. The fact that in the later years of Frost's life he turned his attention to me made for a little uneasiness between Teddie and myself; but we did not know what was on his mind. Robert Frost was the greatest of my teachers because he was the most worldly: only he did not seem to be surprised or daunted by my growing into a dual life.

I would have been lucky enough to have one such mentor; but good fortune brought me a second. Arthur Thornhill came from the publishing side. He was president of Little, Brown and Company, and he was as different from Robert Frost as poetry is from publishing.

My publishing weakness (no doubt reflecting my hesitations about "competing" with my father in poetry) had always been my tenderness about open competition. Arthur, in the years I knew him, took me in hand and encouraged me to compete in the marketplace in my own right. I had never met the man until shortly after my arrival at the Atlantic Monthly Press in 1956, when I was introduced to him at lunch by Seymour Lawrence. Arthur was owlish looking, poised, courteous, piercingly bespectacled, and stunningly direct.

"I'm pleased to meet you, Mr. Davison. I'm sure you're a very good addition to the Atlantic Monthly Press and the whole setup, and I must say I'm glad you've taken the job.

But I wouldn't be honest if I didn't tell you that I advised Mr. Lawrence here against hiring you. He told me you had stood up for him at his wedding. That's a terrible reason to hire a person."

I was absolutely enchanted. The man's frankness amounted to genius. He never, or not more than once or twice with me, carried his candor to the point of discourtesy, though he could be brusque indeed with his closest colleagues at Little, Brown, but his attention, once he had taken a shine to you, was as invigorating and inspiriting in its way as Robert Frost's.

Arthur had been a publisher (like his father before him, and his son after him) for some forty years when I first knew him, and he logged more than half a century before he was through. He began as a boy in the Little, Brown shipping room where his father worked, and in time rose to salesman, sales manager, and executive. At forty-nine he had suffered a serious heart attack, but achieved a complete recovery through good care and good sense. Four years later he became president of Little, Brown. He was sixty-one when I first met him and would stay in harness till the last minutes of his life in 1970. During these years I got to know him better and better. We talked business, mostly over lunch. The Atlantic Monthly Press has published its books jointly with Little, Brown since 1925 under a contractual arrangement with great advantages for both firms—though the two are completely separate concerns, separately owned and managed.

As a consequence of his heart condition, Arthur followed an unusual schedule. Rising at five-thirty to arrive at his office before eight o'clock from his home an hour south of Boston, he put in a good morning's work and then lunched, just after noon, with an author or colleague. Lunch took a long time. Arthur enjoyed three to five glasses of Canadian

Club before getting down to the omelet or calves' liver or scrod. At two-thirty or, more often, three, he returned to his office for an hour and then went home. Since he never went out on business in the evening, he made up for it with his famous lunches. Few tried to match his lunchtime drinks, and those who did regretted it; but even a pair of Bloody Marys in such company could be exhilarating, and in the later reaches of lunch the lettings-down of the hair could become a bit muzzy, the plans for future action could take on a lopsided majesty. Arthur's staff learned to present him with hard decisions in the morning hours.

There was nothing but virility in Arthur Thornhill's constitution, yet he reminded me a little, as he looked shrewdly down his long nose through his glasses, of my grandmother. I could joke with him as I had joked with her—when I could get a word in edgewise. But after the initial jocosities, Arthur would spread out his chronicles of the publishing business, disclose the details of recent negotiations, analyze the character of the presidential eminences whom he had to deal with at other firms, recount in a confidence that I never thought of violating some of the intricacies of his own firm, the jousts, the miscalculations, the successful and the misguided sallies of his subordinates, his happy and unhappy experiences with authors.

Such tutelage made competition human, a matter of contact sport, not savagery. It was possible to work by a man's side without liking him, to contest a negotiation without crippling your opponent. Arthur, who had left school in his teens, believed passionately in books, even though he was usually unable to speak articulately about his particular preferences. He understood the humanity of authors better than their works. He took it as his job to hearten authors by encouraging the businesslike publication of their books and helping to earn them money, but it was the book that counted in the end. He could not disguise his animal confidence that his mission as a publisher was valuable to the world, and he sought to make it profitable to those engaged in it, to the author as well as the publisher. He warned younger colleagues that they would never grow rich in publishing, though he was generous about raises and profit sharing for the best people on his own staff. He himself died a multimillionaire.

Arthur's stated beliefs were simple enough: "honesty," by which he meant saying what he thought ("I'm not *smart* enough to be dishonest"); "fairness," by which he meant getting the most the traffic would bear; and "being a part of something good," by which he meant publishing—in the most profitable way—the best books his editors could direct him to. Like most men who really understand the nature of money, he recognized how the irrational behavior of money reflects the irrational behavior of men.

He had become a connoisseur of human experience, with a vast and hilarious stock of stories drawn from decades of acquaintance with wholesalers, colleagues, competitors and authors. Some of his strangest stories recounted his travels as a young salesman to exotic outposts of the book trade. On one swing through Iowa, with his trunk full of books, he had encountered not only a plague of locusts but an antediluvian doctor who insisted on "cupping" him as treatment for a cold. His talk was punctuated with grins, stares, and very few pauses.

"Am I boring you?" he would ask before launching into a repetition of an old story. It was not easy to get him to turn back, even if, yes, one had heard it before, several times. A demurrer only challenged Arthur to make it new, to add refreshing embellishments. "So he ordered a Bloody Mary. I said, 'Why are you ordering a Bloody Mary? You know you always drink a martini with lemon peel. Is something bothering you?' And he said, 'No, Arthur, it's just I've been getting a little tired of gin lately, is all.' So I said, 'Well, you've drunk enough of it to get tired of it.' And this . . . is true. So I said, 'If you'd of drunk a little less gin and paid a little more attention to the younger people in your operation, you wouldn't be in this pickle, you and the whole setup.' 'You're right, Arthur,' he said."

People always agreed that Arthur was right. They had little alternative. But he usually *was* right. He had a wicked eye for self-importance, for people who got too big for their boots; and although he enjoyed receiving praise as much as anyone, he had earned more of it than most. He was a life-giver because he was more *himself* than other people. Like Robert Frost, he had found his feet relatively late in life, and the configurations of his personality, arrived at in his forties, did not alter much thereafter, though they became more emphatic. Arthur's heart attack had threatened to finish his career until he learned to live with his limitations in middle life, at the age when many other men were burning out or turning corrupt. Also like Frost, he had the ability to spur energy in others, especially in younger men, who would come away encouraged and emboldened. He seemed to be in touch with his own innerness, and the harmony that resulted produced the overflowing vitality of his old age, which he shared freely with authors and publishing colleagues alike.

His wisdom in the end derived not from any unusual analytical capacity but from a sandbur memory in accumulating the results of experience. His gusto, his partisanship, and his favoritism had led him over the years into many mistakes of judgment in assessing people; but he never made the same mistakes twice. He was frank in admitting his own errors and usually as generous in forgiving other people's as he was in giving them credit for their victories. "I don't like people who don't make mistakes." Errors and successes alike took their place in the circus parade of his memory and were trotted out like new floats at the next lunchtime.

But most of Arthur's yarns illustrated such modern challenges as adjusting to reality, meeting the competition, keeping up with change. Though he invariably looked the picture of conventional Boston respectability in his Locke hats, his Brooks Brothers suits, his glowing shoes, he was always a bit ahead of his time in the business of publishing.

5.

Frost and Thornhill set me examples of unity and discipline. Both had immense vitality to direct, both had liberated it by containing it. What of my own life, especially the relative importance of publishing and poetry? Which was to take first place? As I learned more about both writing and publishing, the familiar absolutes tugged at me in both directions. How could I support myself and my family as a poet? How could I banish poetry from my life now that I had unearthed it, a need as urgent as the need for food, sex, sleep? I could not deny the importance of publishing to me as a way of affecting the world, of serving the constituency of letters and not only myself, of living the life of action. What I must learn more about, beyond poetry and publishing, was the nature of commitment.

I gradually discovered that beyond the needs which both writing and publishing satisfied lay a deeper conviction that I could not and should not settle for one or the other. I would have, I thought, to live two lives at once. It was not the outcome I had expected, but I recognized it as mine, for it grew out of the wary self-confidence that arose from my new self-knowledge. If I had a destiny, this was it. To accept its necessity was my second important adult decision, and it came almost simultaneously with my first: resolving to marry my wife. Both seemed to have been handed down, not as an order but as yet another gift.

All the old men whom I admired most were pleased that I was willing to take the risk of following two callings. Arthur Thornhill's understanding of poetry was slender but respectful, yet he knew that two strands could be stronger than one. My father knew from his own experience that the wrong kind of compromise between poetry and the outside world could be fatal. And Robert Frost had in our conversations actively and explicitly encouraged duality.

> I shall be telling this with a sigh
> Somewhere ages and ages hence:
> Two roads diverged in a wood, and I—,
> I took the one less traveled by,
> And that has made all the difference.

Frost's treacherous poem was often "understood wrong." When I thought really hard about it, I noticed that the poem's speaker "knows" certain things:

> And sorry I could not travel both
> And be one traveler . . .
>
> Yet knowing how way leads on to way,
> I doubted if I should ever come back. . . .

But I "knew" no such thing! All my inner experience taught me these assumptions were untrue, that there was nothing to be "sorry" about. I had been back to the same crossroads over and over again in my dreams, and I could be sure of coming back again. Why shouldn't I "travel both and be one traveler"? My youth had been blighted by my insistence on confining myself to one road when my nature was dual. After the years of confusion I decided I could be one traveler *only* if I could travel both roads, the Thornhill way and the Frost way, the Guermantes and the Swann. "The Road Not Taken" should be read like a poem, not a motto. It has been misread (like many other great poems) precisely because as a poem it imposes an artificial solution on a false dilemma and then elicits true poetry from the delusion that results, like a hen brooding on a china egg. The wistful speaker in Frost's poem assumes he cannot travel both roads, but I am certain that Frost himself, with the cunning of his later life ("Yuh gotta make shift") knew otherwise.

When Seymour Lawrence invited me to join the Atlantic Monthly Press in 1956, he must have known me well enough to sense my scruples about competition. I knew him well enough to be sure that he had none, and felt that would make us a good team. At first he asked me for literary advice; later on, as the staff and the list both grew, he delegated much of the administrative work to me instead. As I found I could master it and also became fairly successful in leading new authors to the publishing list, his attitude toward me became suspicious. I found it hard at first to admit that our relationship was deteriorating, for I had other problems on my mind, but once Lawrence's attitude became unmistakable, I was forced to choose between standing up to him or backing away. This time I stood my ground. He left *The Atlantic,* and I inherited his job. The eventual outcome benefited us both, but there is no point in pretending that the process was not accompanied by animus on both sides. I imagine he, like me, feels the scars on gray days.

As so often happens, once I had made my inner decision, outside events resolved themselves with interesting simultaneity. My first book of poems, *The Breaking of the Day*, was chosen by Dudley Fitts for the Yale Series of Younger Poets, and was published in early 1964. A few weeks later I was asked to take over the directorship of the Atlantic Monthly Press. I was thirty-five, a "younger poet" but no longer really young, yet I would often, for a long time, feel woefully inexperienced and it would be some time before I could feel any certainty about my judgment as a publisher or my talent as a poet. I would often despair at what seemed a dual burden, until I remembered that dual vision went with it.

Still, there was a thing or two to celebrate. My daughter Lesley had been born only a few months before all these sudden changes, and my father came to Boston for a long-anticipated patriarchal viewing of the infant, by coincidence, on the day I was asked to take over the Press. Teddie took Jane and me to dinner at Locke-Ober's restaurant in Boston, where, remembering perhaps the ceremonial nature of our dinner together on my eighteenth birthday, he ordered a "fine mutton chop" and a bottle of Pontet Canet. For almost the first occasion in a generation, my father and I were able to talk as equals in fatherhood, poetry, and self-mastery, with the respect two dear friends can have for one another, in full awareness of one another's weaknesses and evasions. He was approaching the last years of his academic career and the end of his good health. He knew that most of what lay ahead was now in the hands of me and my children. Since the occasion seemed to call for it, he made a few "official" remarks, characteristically rummaging among the ruins of the English language for phrases that might for a moment ennoble both speaker and listener. "Lord, now lettest Thou Thy servant depart in peace, according to Thy word. . . ." However inappropriately the psalmist's blessing applied to our own small affairs, Teddie's voice made the *Nunc Dimittis* glow with joy after what we had been through and resignation in the face of what was to come.

Epilogue

Second Growth

We assumed that the man himself
Or someone he had to obey
Wanted us to get down
And walk the rest of the way.

Robert Frost, "The Draft Horse"

The field is studded with their thousand lives.
All that is left of all that tracery
Pokes through the goldenrod in amputations
Too short to see, too tall to be mown over.
Their knuckles sprout new fingers every April.
I go my rounds in August trimming them back.
The roots, now elderly, are just as far
Involved in growing as they ever were,
But their suckers are sickly and cannot survive
Unless they're given help by God or me.

After a year or two of this flirtation
I snap trees off by hand which saw and axe
Once needed all their edges to bring down.
Reason could lull these lives to a merciful end,
But I as owner claim the dark indulgence
Of giving them a chance to sprout once more.
Crops like mine are not so much planted as buried.

P. D., "Stumps"

1.

For American middle-class men, forty is a difficult anniversary, the day we awake to find ourselves no longer in any real sense young. Athletes and mathematicians are considered veterans at thirty and old men at thirty-five. Some can postpone the climacteric for a few years longer, but by the age of forty most men are beginning to feel squeezed from both sides, the past and the future. In the simplest of terms, their parents are approaching the end of their days, and their children will soon be looking, if not acting, like adults.

The changes that take place at forty are not all emotional. A shortness of the breath, an alteration in the eyesight, a fragility of digestion combined with a tendency to overweight, a quickness of temper, a transformation though certainly not a cessation of the sexual appetite—all these are clear physical signs of aging which at forty can no longer be laughed off even by a Pancho Gonzales or a George Blanda. Even so, the severest changes for most men fall in the emotional category. Doctors, psychiatrists, lawyers are all familiar with the sudden changes in desire, the urges for new commitment, that strike most men in the years around and after forty: the sudden divorce after years of contented marriage; the worker who begins reporting imaginary aches and pains;

the competitive businessman who drives himself harder than ever, as though more tension, more pressure, more exercise could dispel his feeling of being pressed or exhausted or fat. S. N. Behrman writes that old age is like being in a room whose walls are closing in, that in old age things take longer and longer to do. This is not so in the middle years, when life in some ways gives us a recess. Despite the waning of some of our energies, the mastery of our skills and experience makes many things easier to do than they have been before, but the world demands more and more from the middle-aged. Our work competes more keenly against our private life. Our communities and our professions badger us for our time and our dedication. Young men, growing eager for our places, begin to press us from below. Those of us who can move up do so. Lawyers become judges, doctors become professors of medicine, workers become foremen, and foremen become superintendents. Fathers become grandfathers, and middle-aged children have to support, or refuse to support, their parents who are retiring from work. We are needed so badly in middle age by so many people that it would obviously be selfish to think of taking any time for ourselves.

Yet there may be no stage in life when it is more important to pause. We have our fully trained minds to draw on, not to mention half a lifetime of experience, and enough energy is still left to change ourselves if we choose. To get this far was half the battle, but not to pause and survey the field could mean losing the war. Yeats wrote, "The innocent and the beautiful/Have no enemy but time." We who are in the middle of life, who are surely past innocence and probably past beauty, can think of time, for a while, as our friend.

At forty we look around for ways to alter, but the old signposts have faded. Change looks both overtempting and appealingly dangerous. We think about changing commitments, about renouncing our hard-earned authority for the sake of new knowledge or self-understanding; or we may consider coming to terms with the values of the younger generation, to strive for religious or ethical understanding, to recover the capacity to learn and listen. Alas, more often than not the change of commitment is only a change of jobs; the renewal of love only a change of partners. Instead of learning to listen we may well end up shutting our ears as well as our mouths. Many middle-aged men waste themselves in a callow contest with youth on its own terms, a game they are bound to lose. Perhaps they *want* to lose. Some encourage youth to rebel because they never rebelled against their own parents. Worse still, some try to quash youthful rebellion, out of a horrible need to defend the status quo simply because it is *ours.* And a great many of us try to play the hero's part just because the hour is growing late, hurrying forward to avoid the pain of looking back.

At forty I am just like everyone else, discontented in spite of everything. I am resentfully taken ill with petty ailments of the skin and the chest and the lower back and the bowel. I rush to work early in the morning and keep it up till late at night. Four hours after I have fallen asleep (when I *can* fall asleep), I wake up again and go back to work. When I do sleep I dream of helpless animals, and when I wake I gaze on my sleeping wife and imagine it is she of whom I have dreamed, that she alone is getting older. I imagine there must be ways to retain my youth, to find a new way of life, a new woman, a new career, a move, a fresh start, a way of being a hero. After a week of nerveless depression I exert myself once again with a manic rush, calling on a "youthful" source of energy that never existed, then or now.

At the moments when my head is clear and my mind fresh I realize how much survives only inside my mind, in no other place on earth, things that only I am in a position to remember, only I can possibly know or imagine. I have developed skills and arts peculiar to me alone—a particular way of editing a book, a special way of speaking in public or reading aloud, a way of persuading, a manner of loving, a style of poetry. I sometimes feel as though I had only just begun to grow, but this is a second growth, as though my destiny now lay not in stretching but in deepening. I am approaching control of the present at last, but in my writing I explore the curious anomaly of "pretending to be asleep," something we do as children when we think our parents are watching, something it is possible to go on doing all our lives.

At forty a new sinister sense of the past was forced on me. The footsteps at my back belonged to the dead. The people who had taught me and populated my dreams began to die, as my mother, Robert Frost, and all my grandparents had already died.

In September 1967 Charlie Morton, the endearing eccentric who had heartened and entertained all his fellow editors at *The Atlantic,* died while traveling in London, aged sixty-seven. In March 1968 Edwin O'Connor, the Atlantic Monthly Press's most successful single author, a witty and companionable man who had strolled in and out of my office almost every workday morning for years, dropped dead of a stroke at the age of forty-nine. Three months later Frank Herbert, who had recently succeeded to the office of publisher of *The Atlantic* after years of training for it, was hauled down in his mid-forties by a ravening cancer. This same year Eugene Reynal, my old boss at Harcourt, Brace, dropped dead, as did Tom Wilson a few months later, and Dudley Fitts, to whom I had become close in recent years, not long after that.

Arthur Thornhill, now chairman of Little, Brown, went

on rollicking into his seventies, but he did not prevent his formerly independent firm from being bought out and turned into a subsidiary of Time, Inc. My father, at seventy, had become ill—not fatally ill, but not likely ever to be wholly himself again. Neither Arthur nor my father now had more than two years to live: they would die within a month of one another in early 1970.

In adolescence it had been my elders, these dying men, who stood between me and my freedom. Now I knew myself to be alone, a tree standing by itself after the loggers had felled the rest of the forest. A man of forty comes to realize that the vast majority of the human race is now younger than himself.

2.

In my fortieth year, 1968, there seemed to be young people everywhere, all of them angry, many of them angry with their elders. In public, as in private, it was the year of deaths and entrances. The young, both on the television screen and in the streets near my Cambridge house, seemed suddenly very different from me (or from any *me* that I could remember), more impatient, readier to act their anger, glad to blur the edges between the inside and the outside of their heads with violence, or with drugs or with music.

The young had become strangely self-conscious (Lord knows we had encouraged them in that!) and I found myself unable to make much of their preoccupations. The only time I tried marijuana I took too big a dose and felt poisoned. I fell into a sleepless, disoriented panic as frightening as my isolation on the Crestone Needle; the drug separated me from people, from my senses, from the world. My two ears worked independently of one another, my toes felt like sausages. After fifteen minutes I lost all sense of the passage of time. (Nothing to count on! Nothing to measure by!) As I slowed down the world speeded up. Yet the experience, shaking as it was, left a curious aftertaste, as though the senses had been washed.

Cambridge in the summers of 1968 and 1969 attracted the uprooted youth of the nation—saffron-robed followers of Krishna; black-clad harbingers of the apocalypse; apostles of various kinds of love, carrying guitars or dulcimers; hashish-breathing grubbies who jammed the benches of the Cambridge Common at night or stood around in crowds in the afternoons, scratching and jouncing; potters and jewelry makers; vendors of broadsides; dealers in drugs.

Harvard itself nearly split apart under the force of the strife among rival student groups protesting the Vietnam war. The faculty was torn away from its laboratories and its studies to argue endlessly about the university's role in a changing society, what Harvard should do to build a new world. The radical students seized the administration building, the police were sent for, heads were bloodied. The whole university now went on strike to support the radicals. In the months that followed there were bombs, stone throwing, shootings, fires, explosions, tear gas in the streets.

I can't pretend to have felt at home in this Cambridge. Though I must have been regarded, walking through Harvard Square in my suit and tie and vest, as yet another baleful member of the War/Hate establishment, all I felt was bewilderment and distaste, impotence and little partisanship. Such rebels as I came to know were among the moderates; only one, the son of an old friend, was a real fire breather, but in due course he left the Weathermen and retired safely to a rural commune. I realized with surprise that youth, while I

was otherwise occupied, had become *them;* but only yesterday youth had still been *us.* How dismaying. There was so
much to do, did I really want to be part of a revolution? Who
would look to my responsibilities if I were? Nobody else
would be likely to bother with all those lives of mine, all
those categories of obligation.

The young faced us with an unanswerable accusation: if
your life had been well spent, the world might be a better
place than it is. Yet though I couldn't fail to hear the call to
leap forward and change society, to take "action," to be
"active," I could not understand where the action was supposed to be leading, nor make out what all the voices were
saying. "Silence is the right action for the alienated artist."
"Yes, he's a reformer and a liberal, but he doesn't *act.*" I
knew neither what was meant by such statements nor what
was wanted.

Young people assume, of course, that each one of us has
absolute freedom of choice, that we can change the world
into any form we wish if we will only try harder. It is the way
I felt at seventeen when I condemned my parents for being
unhappy.

3.

At forty I must have noticed that there were not many
avenues left for change—if not for society, how many fewer
for me! I would never be a hero. I assessed myself, a few days
before my fortieth birthday, in a notebook entry headed
"Dangerous Thoughts":

When I think about my dedication as a publisher, I sometimes wonder how courageous I can ever allow myself to be.

Striking through the veil that divides the present from the future is not an image that describes what I have tried to do, either as a publisher or as a poet. As an editor I have been concerned almost always with the art of the possible, for I have not been blessed, or cursed, with the vanity that enables an Alfred Knopf to project his judgments into the future. I have concerned myself with our present, not with shaping our future by ideas whose time has not yet come.

As a poet I have found it enough, or even too much, to wrestle with the puzzle of my own existence, to keep up with the tide of events and pressures, to embody myself. Not for me— not yet if ever—the attempt at a Supreme Fiction, or to express the conscience of my race, or to chronicle a region or a class or even a milieu. . . .

Yet beyond both "poetry" and "publishing" there is something else, an entity whose outlines I cannot guess at, to which I truly owe allegiance. It lives in the faces of my children, in the touch and sound of my wife, in the knifelike obsessions of unfulfillment, in the dream of the island (or whatever that has now become), in the guerrilla engagements with poetry, in the fury of perfection with the office, in the losing struggle with my life.

There was nothing to brag about in such a formulation. Its limitations were those of place, of class, of education, of possibilities ticked off. I had invented or accepted, long ago, a life of service to a group of vassal identities among which freedom had room only to play a game of power politics, pitting the publisher against the poet, the father against the lover, the lover against the publisher, the poet against the father. At forty, I was forced by the world around me to confess that I had stretched as wide as I could. From here on my changes would have to go in the direction of deepening. Perhaps I could get to the center of my ruling identity and try to heal the divisions in myself.

4.

In 1966 I had been elected an alumni trustee of my old school in Colorado, Fountain Valley. Since it was the only time I have ever been picked for anything by ballot, it seemed prudent to accept the nomination. I got off the plane in Denver for my first board meeting and rented a car to drive south past Colorado Springs, some seventy-five miles. How strange to drive through this half-familiar country, as clear as a stage set, with a new dusting of snow on the ground in May and the air tasting as sharp as blackberries.

The school buildings, like any place not seen since boyhood, looked smaller and lowlier than I had remembered them, but the surrounding plains were as vast as ever. Several of my old teachers were still serving on the faculty, and they looked exactly the same after twenty years. It was only the boys who looked younger. I could not sleep for the thinness of the air and the sharpness of the light at dawn. The air was so dry that my skin began to itch and scale, and I remembered how the woodwork in our Boulder house had always cracked in wintertime for the lack of moisture in the air.

After the trustees' meeting I drove to Boulder to visit one of *The Atlantic*'s authors, and I took the opportunity to call on my old German teacher, Mrs. Kempner. Her house had grown darker as the blue spruce outside her front window had spread to cut off the light and the view of the mountains. The walls of her house had filled up with the bas-relief panels she carved. The little upright piano's brass candlesticks still gleamed through their verdigris. She and I embraced with fervor. (A year later her husband, the old mathematician, wrote me a noble letter describing her death.) In my strangerliness, Boulder seemed curiously changed below its unalterable screen of mountains. Streets were narrow that had once seemed broad; I drove in a short time along mountain roads that had once seemed endless.

In the spring of 1968 my mother's uncle, Fred Herzog, the last tie with Saint Louis, died at ninety-four. Unlike the others who died that year, he was senile, almost blind, childless after half a century of retirement. Part of the money he had meant to leave my mother now descended to me. I found, only forty-five minutes from Boston, in the old colonial parish of West Gloucester, a bare salt-marsh farm of twelve acres with a trim little toylike house. The land also held a large tumble-down barn, a small stand of beech trees, a granite cliff along the southern boundary, and a tidal salt-water creek. There had been a house and a barn on the property probably since before the American Revolution, and there were plenty of signs (smoked and heat-split rocks, half-hollowed fireplaces and caves) of inhabitation by the Conomo Indians long before that. The Indians had probably camped there in summertime to gather clams and mussels from the rich Essex marshes nearby.

Jane and I fell in love instantly with the square shape of the pale yellow house, its softly fluted white Greek Revival pilasters at the corners, the delicate shape of the rooms inside, and especially with the lie of the land.

On the day we took over formal ownership of the house I saw a mockingbird perched on a bough of the old pear tree. My children, pale city creatures wary at first of the bees, skulked close to the house or the car on their first two or three visits, but once they became used to the space, they seemed to take the pasture and the woods for granted and grew as green as their surroundings. I spent two summers clearing the fields. My past and my future began to come together here on this plot of land, as though I had been preserving my past until I found space enough for it.

5.

In early 1970 I lost both Arthur Thornhill and my father. Arthur suffered a fatal heart attack one day in Locke-Ober's restaurant during his first drink before lunch. It would be nice to think that his last words were "Am I boring you?"

My father's death three weeks later was less stylish. For four years he had been suffering from cirrhosis of the liver, brought on by forty years of whiskey, but he had cheerfully observed a strict regimen ever since his first attack and had stayed fairly well, though subdued and sleepy. His second marriage had at last brought calm to his life. He dealt effectively, till his normal retirement, with his duties as Dean of General Studies at Hunter College.

Though he was helplessly saturated with literature and read voraciously through cataract-dimmed eyes till the end of his days, he did not lead a literary life any longer. He wrote nothing except for the last flicker of autobiography that I have quoted. He kept few literary friends, although his devotion to Jack Priestley, and Jack's loyalty to him, remained unchanged. His life turned more and more inward, but there, behind his weakening eyes and inside his sallow unhealthy body, his life still hummed with remembered poetry.

As Teddie lay dying in the all too familiar rooms of Mount Sinai Hospital, I came down whenever I could from Boston and tried not to say my last good-bye at the end of each visit. I brought him the first copy of my latest book of poems, *Pretending to Be Asleep,* and our last real conversation revolved around it. When the final desperate operation was performed I arrived too late to talk to him again: my next-to-last good-bye would have to serve. While we sat together with my stepmother for eight hours of the death watch in the hospital waiting room, Lesley told me that his delirious voice had babbled poems upon poems, nursery rhymes, Shakespeare, verses she had never read or heard before, fragments from the poetry on which his young manhood had nourished itself and which had served him in the solitudes of his life. It was as though one of my nightmares had become real. I had dreamed of my father's corpse being drawn through city streets or burned in the polluted air while the streets teemed with beckoning women. Now, when I carried his carefully prepared obituary to *The New York Times*, the midtown streets were still crowded with prostitutes, though it was noon on Sunday.

My father had loved my Gloucester property: it satisfied his nostalgia for the land and reminded him of the days when he and his young wife and children had lived in the country. He and my stepmother often came to stay in the house. At his express wish, we scattered Teddie's ashes from the granite cliff on my Gloucester property overlooking the salt marshes. He left me his books and papers. I spent the best part of a summer reading through the clippings, the correspondence, the reviews, the diaries and dilemmas of a lifetime, before depositing everything that seemed worth saving in the Yale University Library. It was during this melancholy period, and as I was writing an elegiac poem ("Dark Houses") in his memory, that I began to feel the need to set down the particulars of my parents' gifts to me.

I had been something of a slave to the past, dragging it around with me like my grandfather's made-over suits that I wore all through college. This sort of past is like the old toys we have stored in the attic and can't bear to throw away, like the books we have bought but have never read. Shuffling all those family papers, my parents' love letters, the drafts of poems, the literary correspondence, all the things that have been kept because somebody might still one day want to use them, made me realize I had forgotten my parents, had even forgotten myself. How much truth had slipped between the crevices of the years? My mind, like many men's in middle age, was clearly turning back to my origins, now that death had wiped out so many other people's funds of memory: I had better set down what my own memory offered me while I could still trust it.

The sadness and depression that hung over me could be dispelled, I began to think, only if I could make my mind reach back without suffering the slippages of nostalgia. Yes, my life had been a struggle, like most people's, but what had I been struggling for, and with whom? My parents had launched and piloted my childhood, but now they were unable to ask anything more of me. They had initiated me into love, hate, and most of the desires that furnish my life. What I had done with all those gifts was more my affair than theirs and might turn out to be more my children's affair than mine. Which of my decisions, how much of my identity was really my own? Which had been foreordained? Could I learn enough from my past to face the second half of my life afresh? Or would the descent into memory merely afford a way of escape?

The sheltering presences of my childhood had now given way to their imaginary counterparts, the dark Presences of my unconscious; the Magus, the nourishing mother, the dark city, the bleeding baby, the far island, the young man with a cudgel, the soprano poet with his lyre. Though I had been able to make myself understand them partially, such symbols are never wholly comprehensible. They have a life of their own, they are immortal and dangerous. I would do better to fix on my empirical past, the persons, houses, and presences which "fastened me flesh." "How can I keep in touch," I wrote, "when there is nothing to touch?" Only through the mediation of memory could I perhaps understand a little about Time, could I see in the flesh whatever is visible of God.

My children sometimes asked questions about my past, but they were inquiring for legends. Their lives would be colored by the experience I could describe to them until they grew old enough to look back at my experience with their own perspective. I had no wish to pass on to them the undigested food of my past, to make them in my old age do my understanding for me. It was time to make a retreat. Arrangements for a leave of absence were made at *The Atlantic*. My wife decided on Rome as the place where we and the children would take our year away. We sailed from New York for Naples, and as the days of the sea passage ticked off one by one, I felt as though I were sinking into a dream beyond the reach of time.

6.

As I concluded my research and reflection in Rome and made ready to begin writing this book, I had another of those dreams which, like the handful I have recounted, told me unsuspected things about my own attitude to my own life. From the moment it began I knew it was important. I said to my dreaming self: *I am dreaming. I do not choose to wake up.*

I was a passenger on a ship bound for the United States

across the Atlantic. As I walked on the deck I carried on a lighthearted conversation with a friend. After a time I found myself alone. The ship was now asleep, the portholes were darkened. I was between decks. Somewhere below along a passage tinkled the sounds of a party. As the ship steamed forward I could see out of the port side a field of Roman ruins, some columns standing and some fallen, but all broken or cut short. I knew they were out of my own past.

The ship forged into the darkness, and I had the clear choice of continuing to stand by the porthole surveying the ruins as we passed; or of turning back against the motion of the ship; or even of advancing towards the bow, under my own power, in support of the ship's course. After reflecting a moment I deliberately chose to advance. It was, profoundly, a choice, one which involved difficulty; but it was a free choice. I was not being forced forward by any power outside myself, it was nothing I *had* to do.

I began to advance step by step down the corridor towards the bow. When I came to the end of the corridor I had no choice but to stop or turn right. I turned right. Then, when I reached the end, I turned right once more, toward the stern. No matter what direction I took relative to the ship's motion, every slow pace was an effort, requiring strength and will. Throughout this consecrated progress I knew I could awake if I wished, but I preferred to stay asleep. Not until my final direction was settled, and my dream self was walking slowly back towards the stern of the moving ship, did I wake up.

Unlike the landmark dreams of my youth, this dream carried no alarms or stupefactions, but it seemed to signal a new kind of relationship with my own unconscious. There was no challenge here to life itself, no crushing weight from the outside world, no threats of immense heights, no danger of drowning or being swallowed up. This dream opened like a flower to understanding, to choice, to perseverance, to poetry. I was being informed out of my own depths that the time had come to choose, to gather strength to move and change. I had boarded that ship for a journey of limited duration only. The ruins of the past could tell me only that they existed and that I had explored them. My task done, I must stay aboard the darkened ship and move around in my past, in spite of the motion of the ship towards its future.

Then, nine months later, as I neared the end of this book and began to emerge from my descent into the past, I had a second such dream. I was visiting our old family apartment in New York. As in the shipboard dream, I was accompanied by friends of my own generation, neither of whom had ever met my mother. When we entered the apartment we found her sitting in her former home on a sofa but wearing a hat like a visitor. My dream told me that she had been living separately from my father all the years since her death. She had established herself in a cozy small apartment elsewhere, was working at some useful job, and kept in constant touch with all the kinfolk I had, deliberately or unconsciously, made myself forget about. My father and stepmother were mysteriously absent during this interview, but—even though the apartment had been altered and much redecorated since her death—my mother seemed altogether at home. Her unforgettable laugh chortled out as we talked aimlessly, comfortably. She sat back on the sofa in that soft loose way that she had—I never saw anyone else sit just like that. Though she spoke to me, she would not meet my eyes. It came to me that it was her birthday—the day after the anniversary of her death—and that I had forgotten both dates.

And so I awoke, but she had returned to me in the dream

more wholly than in memory. As I thought about the dream after waking, I imagined she must have been speaking to me, from whatever world dreams take us to, not only on behalf of the spirits of all her dead and forgotten kinfolk, but to aid me in my stumbling effort to reestablish ties with the vanished past.

A friend had written me thirteen years before, after my mother's protracted and horrible dying, that I would forget her death agony and come once again to remember her as she was alive, but that had never happened till now. We all—my father, my sister, my wife, and I—missed her life-giving qualities more than we could have imagined. Though her household had been noisy, quarrelsome, and sometimes desperate, it had been she who drew us together even when our natures drove us apart, just as her mother before her had drawn the disparate and almost incompatible members of her family together by sheer female force on birthdays and anniversaries, to be fed on rare roast beef and buttered carrots in her residential hotel.

Within a year of my mother's dying we all testified to the vitality she had left us: my sister married, my father married again, my wife and I began having children. We all threw out new lifelines, found ways to replace what we had possessed; but in the process of going on we each, not unnaturally, managed to forget something of the quality of what we were replacing.

My mother's family, all those New Yorkers and immigrants whom she went to visit every year on her trips home from Colorado, had all vanished, simultaneously with her, it seemed. (I have hardly seen a one of them again.) So had my sense, never very strong, that New York was our family seat. The city could no longer serve as home to me after her death.

My family has persisted for me only in the posthumous dreams of my mother, which are my dreams because I dream them.

In my childhood we Americans of European descent were all a step closer to the old country than anyone can be now, for that earlier world was wiped out in the second war. My father's mother died in her nineties, and Teddie's last blood relation was his sister, who died of cancer before his own death, leaving him entirely alone of his generation.

In the 1930s, my mother's relations seemed to be everywhere—not only the American-born cousins and aunts; like Isabel, my mother's sister and younger rival for her parents' attention, the wife of a stockbroker living in a Tudor half-timbered stucco house in Scarsdale; or cousin Stanley, who told jokes and conducted public relations for the United Jewish Appeal; or the two ancient black-clad great-aunts, Becky, who sat in crape in a West Side residential hotel and quarreled at a distance with Carrie, who sat in bombazine in Woodmere; or cousin Janet, who ran an East Side dress shop, and her husband Otto. I had forgotten not only all these, but the refugees from Hitler, turning up in New York all through the 1930s, in knots and singly.

These included Alex, the Viennese bank manager in his homburg, moustache, and spats, who could not find a job in America; and his wife Ellie, whose fat little body looked as though she had never eaten anything but Sacher torte; Cousin Rose the contralto, whose very considerable operatic career was cut off at its peak by her exile; Eugene, her dogmatist Catholic husband, who contemptuously sat out the war as a college teacher and returned to the Bundesrepublik as soon as Adenauer surfaced again; Steffi, the pediatrician who could not get a license to practice medicine in the U.S.A. and had, instead, to take up chicken farming in New Jersey;

and others who somehow escaped from Germany and Austria and Czechoslovakia to Brazil, leaving a whole world behind.

As a child I had been just as conscious of the uncles and aunts and cousins who could *not* get out, who thought that it would be safer to stay, like Uncle Albert and Aunt Rosie in Vienna, who were too old to travel, or all the relatives in Czechoslovakia, who were seldom heard from after 1939 and never after 1941. The lone survivor of the holocaust was a woman doctor who converted to Catholicism and managed to keep herself and her children alive in Slovakia till after the war, and who may for all I know still survive, though I can't even remember her name now. The rest of my mother's tribe, the kinfolk whom my grandparents used to visit in central Europe and talk about for years afterwards, have vanished, except for the unidentifiable figures in some un-labeled photographs in an album. Yet when I was a child, all these people were alive, as much in repute as anyone's cousins in Connecticut or Kansas. If the memory of my generation is muddled, it is history, in addition to mental confusion, that muddled it. We forgot some things because we chose to, but in these last oblivions we had no choice.

I find now, in my forties, that it is my motherland, not my fatherland, that I have too deeply neglected. My mother's gifts were not as easily absorbed as those gifts of words which my father gave me. When she died, I must have turned my memory away in revenge for her departure and choked it off in my new ambitions to become a husband and a father, a publisher and a poet.

My mother's gifts? Could the fantasy island of my youth, the land where oranges blossomed, have been transformed into a motherland? No, that youthful place had a different quality. The island's purposes had been divisive; it could not exist without its opposite, the dark city. My mother's country was illuminated by glints of light rather than spoken doc-trines, laughter and tears rather than laws, work that was also play, music rather than words. The joy given and taken in unforced friendship, the generosity that rises easily beyond the self to the needs and natures of others, the gaiety that finds life not always too heavy to lift—none of these was my father's specialty. The powers that gave my mother her grace, even though eventually they failed her, could maybe become mine if I understood them and myself well enough.

My descent into the past has not been undertaken to find out who I was: I already knew that well enough for practical purposes and too well for comfort. My task is to find out what I might have inherited but have forgotten. What lies ahead is to accept what I cannot change; to find freedom in, as well as from, the past. Every child relives his parents' lives in this sense, as though they left him a colorful but tangled yarn which he could spend his life unraveling. If only he can remember more than he forgets!

From now on can I expect to relent in the ambitions which have blindly driven me for so long, and rely instead on the less self-regarding energies of hope, who is always presented in the figure of a woman? Can I rely on the love of giving life rather than in the lust to signify? The desires to transform and restore rather than the urges to possess and define?

My twenties were my age for decision and definition; my thirties were my age for commitment. Later on I shall have to think about passing on what I have inherited, to make my way out of the scene gracefully. Only now, in my forties, am I given the opportunity for renewal. If I succeed, there will be forces in myself that for the first time can be changed into the coin of consciousness, so that I may fulfill my childhood dream of crossing the water and reaching my mother on the other side.

7.

On most mornings now that this exploration is over, I drag myself from bed and dress in business livery: a suit, an overcoat, a slightly ridiculous hat, a briefcase full of paper work that I have tried to finish off after dinner or before breakfast. I leave the house and set out into the lowering February day with the pavement under my feet as cold as cliffs. As I trudge towards the subway train the snowflakes flicker at my cheeks. My body is warming to its task of walking; my mind is mulling over yesterday's unsolved problems; my emotions are calm from the knowledge of my wife's usual love and my children's usual happiness.

As I walk towards work, I know that all these lives of mine occupy a single house, here inside my shirt, in the crabbed present, no matter how far outside time and space they began. From the singing together, quietly at first, of the voices of my lives, I begin to hear a strain which I have never heard before, but which I have never quite forgotten. I overhear, first, a note or two, or perhaps they are words. I hold them in my mind, not fixed, not captive. When I reach a seat on the subway, or a laundromat along the way that has a free chair in it, or the last surviving shoeshine parlor, I may pull out a scrap of paper, sit, and try to scribble in my lap the words that went with the music or arise from it.

It is here that poems begin, not in literature, not in happiness or misery, not in heroism or suffering, but in the very midst of life—between the conscious and the unconscious, between home and work, between childhood and old age, between the city and the island, walking towards the subway on a winter morning after a season in Rome.